SLAYING SOUTHWEST FLORIDA

Curated by Leigh M. Clark

Aurora Corialis Publishing

Pittsburgh, PA

OTHER COLLECTIVES BY LEIGH M. CLARK

Slaying Tampa Bay

Slaying Atlanta

Slaying Nashville

The Dream is in Your Hands

The Dream is in Your Hands: She Can Do It

Living Kindly: Bold Conversations About the Power of Kindness

To all the women who had faith in this project when it was just an idea...

Thank you for being the type of women who support other women and encourage them to follow their dreams. You all deserve to be seen, valued and heard. This book is just the beginning of that mission, and I'm stepping up to make it my priority. I see you, I believe in you, and I will continue to honor you.

With Love and Kindness,

Leigh M. Clark

TABLE OF CONTENTS

Giving Back in SWFL

Alicia Miller-Shannon

Alicia Miller-Shannon is the executive director of Our Mother's Home of SWFL, Inc., whose mission is to empower young women in the foster care and human trafficking systems to break the generational cycle for themselves and their children. She is responsible for overseeing the administration, programs, and strategic planning of the organization. She's also in charge of fundraising, marketing, and community outreach to help support the unique environment for young mothers and their babies.

Alicia graduated from the University of Florida with a bachelor's degree in psychology and a minor in secondary education. She was previously the executive director for The Deaf and Hard of Hearing Center and the adoption specialist for The

Children's Network. Her experience with the foster care system, along with her desire to be a role model and leader for young women, led her to Our Mother's Home.

In 2019, Alicia was named one of Gulfshore Business' 40 Under 40, and in 2020, Alicia was recognized as the Community Foundation's Executive Director of the Year. Alicia is also on the board of directors for The Greater Fort Myers Chamber of Commerce and was listed as one of three APEX Women in Business finalists in 2021 and 2023.

Alicia is a dog-lover, avid reader, and female empowerment enthusiast. She loves American Sign Language! She is also a college football fan and is the vice president of the SWFL Gator Club. She enjoys spending time with her family, French bulldogs, and helping the community.

***

"In a gentle way, you can shake the world."

~ Gandhi

You've read about women *slaying* Southwest Florida, but these women are also *serving* Southwest Florida. This area is home to a thriving nonprofit sector, where organizations are dedicated to making a positive impact in the community. From Fort Myers to Naples, there's a range of social issues to choose from when deciding how to leave an impact. Whether it's environmental conservation, social services, education, healthcare, or the arts, finding your passion and giving back is the best way to fulfill your personal mission and be successful in your journey.

With over 3,500 nonprofits, it's clear that community involvement is a hallmark of Southwest Florida. Residents and businesses alike contribute to these agencies through volunteering, donations, and partnerships. If you aren't sure where to leave your mark, start by focusing on specific issues you want to change. The Conservancy of Southwest Florida focuses on environmental conservation and protecting our unique, natural resources. They play a vital role in safeguarding the ecosystems of our area, like the Everglades, which is critical to Florida's environment.

Then we have Community Cooperative, which serves as a lifeline for residents facing food and housing insecurities. With a mission to eliminate hunger and homelessness, while simultaneously inspiring and supporting sustained positive change in its clients, their impact was crucial during times of crisis, like Hurricane Ian. There's also Golisano Children's Hospital, which provides specialized care to children in need by offering cutting-edge medical services, and the Gulf Coast Humane Society which offers shelter, veterinary services, and adoption programs to find loving homes for animals. And you can't forget Alliance for the Arts, a nonprofit that is enriching our community's cultural life and transforming lives through the arts.

While these larger organizations represent a portion of the nonprofits in Southwest Florida, they illustrate the broad spectrum of causes and issues we are addressing. Additionally, many smaller nonprofits cater to local needs like Hearts and Homes, supporting veterans, and Our Mother's Home empowering teen mothers in the foster care system.

Our charitable region is not without its challenges, though. Fundraising and volunteer recruitment are ongoing efforts, especially in times of economic uncertainty. Transformative events like COVID-19 and Hurricane Ian tried to knock us down, however, the resilience and dedication of these organizations have allowed us to weather many storms, both literally and figuratively. Southwest Florida nonprofits represent beacons of hope and progress in a region blessed with natural beauty and a strong sense of community.

We are a small, but mighty community that shares a sense of camaraderie and purpose and we know how to come together to create change. The women in this book are a driving force behind the success of these nonprofits. They are fueled by passion and commitment and work tirelessly to address the wide array of issues in their community. They not only improve the quality of life for many, but they also serve as a testament to the power of women and communities coming together for a common cause; slaying Southwest Florida.

Opening

Christin Collins

Christin Collins is a magnetic and thought-provoking influencer, a certified workplace mindfulness facilitator and an executive coach. With certifications in holistic coaching, she's an accomplished author and a national speaker who illuminates the path to optimal well-being. Her expertise delves deep into the mind/body connection, the profound impact of trauma healing, and the detrimental effects of stress on the physical body, all while emphasizing the importance of coherence and regenerative practices. In 2022, Christin was privileged to share her transformative message at the TedX Westshore conference in Tampa, Florida.

Having held key roles as a former healthcare executive, Christin served as the system director of health and wellness and senior director of development at a prominent Southwest Florida healthcare system. Her influence extends to her role as vice-chair of the Global Positive Health Institute Board of Directors, and her previous membership in the American College of Lifestyle Medicine Happiness Science & Positive Health Committee.

Christin's programs guide executives, teaching them to harness the power of presence, compassion, courage, and connection within the c-suite. Her practical strategies bridge the gap between corporate ambition and humanity, enabling executives to make informed decisions, communicate effectively, and foster positive attitudes within their teams.

Christin's unwavering commitment to promoting mindfulness and holistic well-being positions her as an invaluable asset to any organization seeking to thrive in compassionate leadership and employee empowerment.

***

Women supporting women.

Women who are comfortable in their own skin.

Women who are *slaying it* at a soul level.

This collection of stories celebrates women in Southwest Florida. These are women who have done the work, who show up with a vengeance, who make things happen. These women have connected with who they are, why they are, and are living their truth.

How did they get here? How did they get to this point in the journey with so many life challenges, plus COVID and two cataclysmic hurricanes?

To answer these questions, I paused and pondered my own journey. I was gifted with the opportunity to introduce these incredible stories. Who are these women who are inspiring and impacting thousands and thousands of lives? The same theme kept emerging as I wrapped my mind around this.

I did the work. I sat with my shit. I pondered. Questioned. Got uncomfortable. Faced a number of things and sat in the emotions that followed. I paused and allowed it all to flow through me. Thanked it all for visiting. Then released it, at a soul level.

For me, life had been pretty darn good. I had a fabulous and kind husband who loved and supported me, and two incredible stepchildren who I cherished and adored. I had one loyal, fun-loving dog, a big house, a fancy car, and a boat. I was a member of country clubs, had achieved professional excellence, and had plenty of friends.

I had built the life of my dreams and appeared to be winning at life... aka "slaying it."

Yet as time unfolded, my health issues expanded, and my well-being declined. This was super confusing because I worked *in* healthcare; I was the executive overseeing health and wellness for a two-billion-dollar company.

I chalked it all up to aging and brushed the health issues off, figuring that my body was just sending me signs that it sucks to get old.

When it comes to slaying it, you have two choices: You can slay it from your ego (head), or you can slay it from a place of authenticity (heart). And I promise you, these are two *very* different approaches.

For decades, I slayed it from my head. From my need to feel good. From my addiction to the dopamine hit I received when I "crushed it." I won awards. Stood on stages. I was in the news and recognized by my community.

I thought I was officially slaying it.

Yet it got to a point where I realized I could not connect with satiation. There was never enough to sustain my satisfaction. It hit me like a freight train that I was constantly chasing after the impact so I could love who I was.

This reality stopped me in my tracks. I had not been loving myself for just being the real *me*: Imperfect, well-intended, somewhat goofy, and definitely inconsistent. Instead, I was making myself earn my own self-love each and every moment of each and every day!

I sure was a whole lot nicer to other people in my life than I was to myself.

So, as said before, I sat with my shit. And turned within.

What came out of this soul-searching was my book, *Her Phoenix Rising*, a reflection of my journey to health and healing through self-love. This book shares hard lessons learned and the letting go that followed. Since birth, I experienced levels of trauma that impacted my safety and development. Years of abuse destroyed my self-worth, and I carried this into my adult life. I was in a constant search for safety and love. I craved approval and made decisions subconsciously based on these deep-rooted events.

Writing this book provided the opportunity to deeply connect with these lessons, release, and heal. This sharing was a gift to myself, as an opportunity to face, embrace, and let go.

But as soon as it was published, I was overwhelmed with fear and self-doubt, questions swirling in my mind:

WHY did you share these stories of shame and vulnerability with strangers?

Who really cares anyway?

How might this impact my career, place in the community, family, and friends?

I sat alone, newly afraid, taking my own medicine. It was time to embrace a new level of healing, supporting the rise of deep authenticity without attachment. I had met myself for the first time. All of me. The good, bad, and the ugly.

Two years later, after quite a roller coaster of emotions, I can report that this sharing changed every single aspect of my life. And I do mean every single aspect. No dark corners. No more fear. No more addiction to what others thought or felt about my journey. Just little ole me. Honest. Open. Calm.

And for the first time ever, I felt at peace.

From this place of wholeness, I welcomed a different approach to *slaying it.*

This soul-level slaying embodies acceptance. Unique perspectives. Forgiveness, empathy, compassion, and love. It uses a lens of infinite possibilities, as well as infinite truths. It is built upon the awareness that every single human alive experiences a very distinct and individual reality.

It embraces the perspective that I am only responsible for one person on this merry-go-round we call life. Just one. I am here to slay *my* journey, from a deep-seated place of love and wholeness.

Slaying it from within, from a place of love, looks and feels different.

It is a surrender. Not a process of blowing your adrenal glands from a perpetual "fight-or-flight" hunt.

It is a pause. Not a sprint as ever-loving fast as you can to get as much stuff done as inhumanely possible.

It is a curiosity. A contemplation. An intuition. A deep knowing.

It is often against the grain. Rarely do I see a bunch of sameness around me. This version of slaying it welcomes being different. Not necessarily being understood. And definitely not following a crowd.

Nor does it entail selling out to entice a crowd.

Nope. It's a slaying it based on love. Differences. Non-judgement. In the comfort of knowing that we are all here to be our divine, unique selves, and see the world according to this lens. That our hardships and mistakes provide the edge to push up against, where we can redirect to reconnect with who and why we are.

Slaying it is not done at the expense of others. Slaying it is showing up deeply connected with our hearts, souls, instincts, and inner knowing. When we slay it from here, we are vibrant. Can't-put-your-finger-on-it attractive. We welcome instead of force. We shift from human *doings* to human *beings*.

In this mode, it's no longer about making the world a better place or trying to change the direction of other people's pathways. Feeling that our way is right, and their way is wrong. It's about welcoming each and every soul to connect with who they are, and why they are, and expecting it to look like a beautiful tapestry, interwoven and interconnected.

This sort of slaying it is flow and calming... yet so freaking powerful!

As you experience this collection of stories, I encourage you to absorb the depth of courage it took for each of these women to share. And not only to share it with you, the reader, but to own and face it themselves. This book celebrates the pause and the ponder, the reflection and the emotions that come with those times that we are called to pause. It also serves as a tool to heal and release.

It's from this depth that each woman continues their journey to support the rising of Southwest Florida and beyond.

This book is a testament to overcoming and shows us the importance of working through it instead of going around it. It is an offering to a part of the planet that is looking to connect with its resilience and support the health and healing of all. Together, we share to honor, to feel it all, and to shed the baggage so that we may each slay our individual journeys with humility and grace.

You have connected with this collection of stories for a reason. I encourage you to welcome the opportunity to be stirred and see what bubbles up for you. It is prime time to connect with this present moment, to let go of the past and the concerns about a future that is not even here yet. To let go of worrying about what others are doing, saying, and experiencing. To connect with who *you* are and *why* you are. To understand your unique, divine pathway. To celebrate diverse and different ways of being, and seeing. And to enjoy the interconnectivity of it all.

The time is now. To be here now, to reconnect with the love that is already inside, is what we are all searching for. This is the exhale and the bliss that we want so badly. It's already here, inside of each of us, ready to be re-connected with. Let these stories stir you to find this within yourself, by sitting in the quiet and embracing whatever bubbles up. Thank it for visiting and kiss it away. If you are ready to truly slay it, simply be Love. Be here now.

Take that next step toward connecting with the love that lives inside of you.

With immense gratitude and love, CC.

From the Wreckage, She Found Freedom

Karina Borgia-Lacroix

Karina Borgia-Lacroix, better known as The Real Estate Title Girl, is the owner and founder of Borgia Consulting Corporation & American Real Title, which has been in operation for over 14 years. It is certified as a 100% woman- and minority-owned business. Along with being a title, closing, and escrow agent, Karina is a real estate expert, consultant, investor, and educator in the field.

Karina was inducted into the Marquis *Who's Who in America* directory for her professional integrity, outstanding achievements in her field, and making innumerable contributions to society. She was recognized as one of 100 Women to Know in America and won the USA's Title Expert of the Year award in 2020 and 2021, as well as the Title Innovator Award in 2022. Karina was named one of the Women of Influence in Real Estate in America and received the 40 Under 40 award by Gulf Shore Business. Karina has been featured in numerous workshops, classes, seminars, magazines, and podcasts around the country. She is always sharing her professional expertise, educating others based on her experience as a business owner, and inspiring others to overcome adversity. Karina's biggest passion and commitment is giving back to her community, and she devotes her free time to volunteering, reading to children in elementary schools, and helping local organizations. Karina is currently a board member for Blessings in a Backpack, has served on many other boards for local charities, and is a current member of a variety of local organizations.

Karina shares her life with her two sons Akai (28) and Levi (10).

***

Where does my story begin? I ask myself that question often, and although specific moments in time come to mind, I am not sure where the story of my brokenness really begins. If you see me, meet me, talk to me, I doubt you would ever question my internal happiness. My perpetual smile, my endless energy, my ambition, and my drive would lead you to believe that my journey has been a perfectly wrapped package of love, peace, and sunshine.

Are you smiling right now, knowing that you too have the same quality? Many of us know how to put that big mask on to hide the pain, to smile when you want to cry. You, too, may have the drive to achieve what society expects of you, only so you can decorate your life with accomplishments and not focus on regret, sadness, and pain. Are these accomplishments really accomplishments, or are they mere bandages for the wounds in our souls?

Human brokenness is the mosaic of shattered dreams, fractured spirits, and a flawed tapestry of our shared existence which forever shapes how we see the world, how we behave, and how we relate to others. If you are reading these words, maybe you too are wondering how much of your own brokenness drives everything you do. Maybe you haven't yet realized it... it took me over 40 years to wake up.

Shame, self-preservation, the need to protect others, and the fear of being perceived as "weak" have kept me from sharing my story until now. Had I shared my brokenness earlier and stopped pretending I wasn't affected by it, I believe my brother may not have felt alone in his pain and maybe would still be alive today.

When did all of this brokenness start? I wondered. In my head, I felt like if I could figure it out, I could turn back time, separate myself from what took place, and stop carrying the weight.

Was it while surfing through a drug-fueled childhood where our home was a prison, where I learned to identify every drug by its smell? Was it watching brutal violence and witnessing death over drug wars? Was it seeing my mother physically beaten, bloody, and crying from my father's own hands? Was it accompanying my father and brother during their countless drug rehab programs and jail visits while watching the many other broken souls?

Maybe it was while helping my mother flee so she didn't have to endure the physical and mental abuse that she would only go back to. Or maybe it was when I ignored my brother's pain so I didn't have to face mine.

Was it the conflicting pain I felt when my father passed?

Maybe it was the heartache I felt and still feel when my brother mysteriously passed three weeks after my father's death, or maybe it was watching my mother's never-ending sadness from the loss of her son.

Perhaps it was a compilation of all these heart-crushing experiences.

At the age of five, I distinctly remember hiding under my bed crying. The marble floor was cold to my skin, and, for some reason, this dark, cold empty space was the only place I felt safe. I couldn't cry to my father as he was creating the pain; I couldn't cry to my mother because I needed to be strong for her. During those crying episodes where every day felt like a storm of fear and uncertainty, I started forming my perceptions of the world, my part in it, and what *not* to expect from it. I began to question God's existence.

All these emotions took place while yearning for safety and a normal, nurturing childhood. I quickly realized I was alone; I would always be alone, and no one would ever save me from the chaos. That my dreams were forever going to be overshadowed by the harsh reality I was facing and that if I wanted out of the chaos, I needed to do it by myself and for myself while detaching all emotions from my world.

As I grew, I carried the weight of my shattered home with me, forever scarred by the chaos that surrounded me, and longing for the chance to break free from the cycle and find solace in a world that seemed so elusive.

Those early years formed what I could barely call a childhood. They shaped me into someone who believed that control was the key to survival. Control was my refuge. It became my armor against the unpredictable. I had watched my parents stumble through a world filled with substance abuse and anger, and I was determined to carve out a different path. But, in my quest for control, I discovered that I was merely trading one kind of chaos for another.

I had always been the one to insist on doing everything myself, convinced that no one else could be trusted to handle my responsibilities. I couldn't bear the thought of leaving anything in anyone else's hands, even if it meant running myself ragged. It was as if control was the only thing standing between me and the abyss.

At 18, I found myself in a situation that would test the very core of my need for control. I gave birth to my first son. In my need for control in the lonely world I had created, I found it hard to accept help and refused it from almost everyone, determined to prove that I could provide for my child on my terms. It was an exhausting journey, working multiple jobs, attending college full-time, and struggling to put food on the table. I wanted to make sure that no one could ever say that my decision to keep my child was a derailment of my future success.

I also became increasingly controlling of my environment.

In my world of control, I was overwhelmed by my need for perfection, exhausted, unable to trust others, and had no ability to be flexible. Although this led to a very high-functioning life where I exceeded my own expectations, I rolled through two failed marriages and became a single mother once again. My need to prove a point to the world that it didn't matter where I came from was so strong that I never assigned any of these failures to my inability to compromise.

I couldn't compromise with anything or anyone—not even myself.

On September 5, 2016, my life was forever changed. I was involved in a near-fatal car accident. Not only was my car hit head-on by a truck, but it also rolled into a water retention area and sank. My two-year-old son was in the back seat. I became unconscious at the time of impact. The driver who caused the accident dove into the water to save me, not realizing that my son was in the backseat. He struggled to get me out as the car was completely crushed on my side and I was buckled in. He decided to give up. All of a sudden, the overhead lights flickered three times. He noticed my son in his car seat and shifted his efforts to try to save him. He successfully saved my son and felt he couldn't leave him without his mother and went back to save me. He removed me from the wreckage!

I suffered memory, hearing, and vision loss. I had 87 staples placed in my skull, my left ear was reattached, and I had water in my lungs. I lost half of my hair and had countless surgeries on my head, neck, and left arm. I was also unable to figure out numbers in my head for almost a year and feared I would never be able to work again. My son had no injuries.

Surviving, paradoxically, didn't bring relief; instead, it brought a haunting awareness of life's unpredictability. The realization that I controlled nothing, that existence itself is a fragile thread cast a shadow over the relief of survival. It was a stark reminder of my vulnerability, leaving me with bittersweet gratitude for being alive, tinged with the painful understanding that I am at the mercy of forces beyond my grasp.

I realized that I had only truly started living once I let go and now appreciate the small, unexpected joys that life offers. It was as if I had been living in black and white and suddenly discovered a world of vibrant colors.

I have learned that true strength lies in the ability to adapt and find beauty in the unexpected. I discovered that control is an illusion, and the real magic of life unfolds when we embrace the uncertainty and unpredictability of the journey. My journey has been a testament to the resilience of the human spirit and the transformative power of letting go, for it is in surrendering to life's uncertainties that we discover the true beauty of the human experience.

I have continued to dissect the brokenness caused by my past, but that journey is now simpler to understand as I realize that life doesn't happen directly to me, it happens around me... I am just here for the ride!

A Beautiful Mess

Talisha Faber

Talisha is known for her exceptional work in the commercial real estate industry, commitment to the community, and expertise in lending from her years in financial services. Talisha has built her reputation as a trusted advisor and community advocate. She serves on the Board of Directors for Our Mother's Home, a local non-profit that provides a safe and nurturing environment for young moms in foster care and their babies and also has been a "Dress for Success" speaker and mentor for many women. Talisha thrives on entrepreneurship and enjoys serving on the Junior Achievement Hall of Fame advisory board, loves being a Rotarian, and most recently was a recipient of the prestigious Woman of Distinction award for her acts of kindness throughout the years. Talisha understands that her role is to take a hand as she climbs up the ladder and show others that, regardless of your circumstances, you can create your own room for others to learn and thrive in.

***

Trying to find the beauty among the mess has always been my strong suit... even if the toilet floods more than half the house as I sit at my desk, completely unaware.

I wish I could begin to tell you about the mess I grew up with and illustrate its beauty as a great gem to add to the collection of stories here—but let's be real: the beauty tends to shine through *after* the cleanup happens.

I was born to teenage parents. My mother (a bartender), and my father (a mason), offered messy opportunities for clean-up on a pretty continual basis. "Loving" and "kind" were always among their best traits, and this has been an ongoing theme throughout my life, as well as their love affair with their family, thankfully.

Alcoholism and drug abuse along with three different sets of stepparents entering and leaving my life were also common themes. So, believe me when I say I understand what "messy" means!

To follow my career in professional dance, I started my journey toward personal growth at a high-end local grocer. I took notice of the hustle and grind that it took to succeed and leave the hood I lived in. I dressed and behaved as someone double my age and experience and literally faked it until I made it.

Boy did I do a lot of that!

As I began to learn some real tools, I also learned the power of knowledge and relationships. I remember one of my employees writing a letter about how my leadership had made an impact on her life. It was then that I realized my calling: I was meant to help that one person who needed someone to believe in them. Just one.

After a successful career as a lender, business banker, and private client manager for Florida and creating a great brand as a community advocate, I was laid off at the beautiful age of 47. Yes, there was that damn mess again! All of this happened after a horrible breakup of my 20-year relationship with my now ex-husband, and after some health issues that I was pretending weren't happening.

Earlier in my life, my faith had been formed from a little white church bus that picked me up, along with my neighbor, Candy (who ironically sent me a Facebook request just this morning).

Among the drinking, the drugs, and the sexual intoxication I was exposed to, I also was given the gift of my own faith that during that messy time. Because of that, I leaned on a higher power to settle myself and own my thoughts when they were scattered throughout my life. That little church bus most definitely kept me from drugs among many other experiences when I was younger.

It turned me into a believer, which is what impact is all about. All you need to do is reach that one person, one believer, who will settle those thoughts of doubt and disbelief about whatever they are going through. For me, the church bus brought me to a place where I realized there was more than just a mess: there was purpose. And I could rise above.

As a full-time single mom, a huge advocate for community service, and a big proponent of women creating their own inheritance and legacies, I believe it's time to sit in the middle of the dirt, be smarter than most in your industry, and grab someone's hand so they can watch and learn from you and the other powerhouses in your tribe. My tribe is your tribe, and believe me when I tell you they don't play small and are beautifully unapologetic about it. Male-dominated industries like commercial real estate (my field), are begging for women to own their affluence.

The world is coming alive because of women who will leave a legacy to their children and communities.

Let's sit in this mess and clean it up together... there's beauty in it.

Destined by Faith

Jessica Diaz

Jessica Diaz has been a resident of Southwest Florida since 2001. She currently resides in Naples with her four children. Jessica launched a successful real estate career in 2013 and has gone on to become a top performing agent in her marketplace. She has a profound love for her community and is an influencer in the lives of many young entrepreneurs and working mothers. Most recently she was featured in Women to KNOW in Florida 2023.

***

"Can I have your autograph?"

This is a strange question to be asked as a 10-year-old girl from Ohio with no celebrity status or international exposure whatsoever. My family packed up their lives and moved to

Moscow, Russia, the day before my 10th birthday to carry out an important calling that would radically change my life forever. I'll never forget the day, it was September 9, 1993, and our plane landed on a chilling Moscow tarmac just shy of 24 months after the prolonged transition from the communist regime formerly known as the USSR to the now Russian Federation. As I walked off the plane, I didn't know it then, but I was stepping into history.

We spent much of our time there on a platform in front of multitudes of Russians, witnessing the joys of their newfound freedom. We were sharing God's message of the gospel and instilling hope and a sense of liberation into their communities, schools, families, and workplaces. It was new for them, yet it is something much of the world so easily takes for granted.

The people of Russia had been very isolated during the Cold War and had just a little exposure to our Western (US) culture. Many of the children had never seen Americans in person—but what they had seen of our culture, music, movies, and lifestyle, they loved. To those children, my siblings and I were like movie stars. It certainly put our comfy American lifestyle into perspective for us.

Missing friends and family back home was a part of my daily life. If I wanted to reach out to anyone back home, I'd have to purchase a calling card from the kiosk down the street, and just talking for a few minutes was costly. I found that the best source of communication was sending handwritten notes via fax. (I know, so dated, but it was cheap and effective.)

We were led by our faith, and we shared our light freely. Our ministry work was empowering, and we served to transform lives from the inside out. My family has a long legacy of affecting change in the world through sharing our beliefs, and it continues on to this day.

My time in Russia over the three years we were there was at times shocking—and overall, it was life-changing. Even as a young girl, the experience was polarizing: on some stages in front of certain crowds, I was treated like a child star; in other situations, because of former communist isolation and propaganda, I was more like the devil. My experience with such unbalanced acceptance showed me how to stand true to who I was and continue to lead with my heart, regardless of other people's opinions or predetermined ideas of me.

When we returned to the United States, our family settled briefly in New Hampshire before we transferred down to Southwest Florida ahead of my senior year of high school. By then, my older brother and sister had gone off to college. My parents helped them financially to get into great schools out of state, and I was very eager for my day to come. I began to think about where I would want to go to college, but I knew after speaking with my parents that they were overextended on education bills, and I would have to find a way to make my college dreams come true. Ministry work is not exactly the most financially rewarding, but it certainly has its other forms of rewards, and I understood then that it was just a way of life.

I was thrilled to have stumbled upon a full ride scholarship program called Bright Futures that picked top students with high SAT and ACT scores—the scholarship would provide people like me with resources to attend a state school. I knew I'd have to pay additional living expenses, but I worked really hard and aced my exams and got accepted into the program.

Knowing my parents had a lot on their shoulders in our thriving community, I strove to do everything I could on my own financially. Being the determined high school student that I was, I saved up enough money to purchase my first car. I was so proud the day I pulled my little white Pontiac LeMans into our driveway.

I swung open the door and called to my parents to come see what I'd accomplished. I thought they'd be so proud. My father circled the car and shook his head in disappointment. The car I was so proud of was, this LeMans, in his opinion, was a lemon. And I was crushed.

In hindsight I realize my father had wanted to be included in the process and help me get a reliable car. I just knew they were already financially strapped and thought doing it all on my own would relieve their burden a little. They had instilled such a strong work ethic in me, I couldn't really help myself. It was a lesson that what was intended and what was received were two very different things.

That was just one of many life-changing moments I faced during my senior year in high school. I had to watch my parents go through a church split, which I've never seen before. The church turned against my family and suddenly became a bunch of nasty people spewing hate at my parents. These people were coming up to me and speaking badly about my family, not knowing I was the pastor's daughter. That was one of the hardest things I had to endure. What made it worse was that, at this point, I was the oldest sibling in the household, and no longer had my own older siblings to turn to for support. I had to carry the weight of watching my dad get maligned by members of the congregation.

My dad has always been someone I've greatly admired and he's always been treated with respect. He's done so much good work for God and worked tirelessly to bring that message to the masses. He takes such good care of our family, especially my mother. They take care of one another in a way that shows God's love. They're such a wonderful couple. And then I had to see God's people severely mistreat this great couple. I had to take that on and try not to let it make me angry. But it did make me bitter and it changed my perception of the church.

Fresh from that experience I went off to the University of Florida. When I first moved to Gainesville, I was burnt and wanted nothing to do with ministry at that point. I was approached by a Christian organization called Chi Alpha. They asked me to participate and be their president. They'd heard all these great things about me and places where I'd been around the world, different ministries and stages that I've been on. They wanted me to participate and be a part of this club at University of US, but I had to refuse.

Still, I thrived in college, and found a new kind of love. I'd go on from there to meet the father of my four beautiful children. A few years after we married, seemed like I was incessantly pregnant—I had four babies in less than five years! My first two children were delivered naturally in the hospital. For the next two, I felt like I'd had enough experience to try giving birth in water in a birthing suite. I decided that this was more aligned with the way I wanted my children brought into the world, regardless of the opinions of others. Each experience was so beautiful and unique in its own right. Digging deep internally and finding peace despite my discomfort or opposition of others was something I knew was instilled in me from a very young age. I was proud of the courage I had to do things exactly as I envisioned, regardless of resistance from others.

I was no stranger to overcoming obstacles to pursue what was right in my heart. I had grown into a woman who knew her strength and determination. When my kids were young, my heart was open to the pursuit of a newfound dream.

Having been part of a family who opened our home countless times to host others during our time in ministry, I was always inspired by hosting and the overall home-making experience. I wanted to purse that passion in my professional life as well. I worked so hard to learn about real estate, despite my spouse's disapproval. The night I went to take my state real estate exam, he really lost it. I could see he didn't really support what mattered to me in my life's journey.

That night was emotional, but it took my mind off the fear of failing the test. I passed it and began a career that I would thrive and grow in. My marriage didn't thrive, but what I'd later realize is that was the career that allowed me to raise my children in a loving and stable home, albeit as a single mom.

Becoming a single mother, trying to do it all, was no easy feat, but through many of my life's experiences, I'd like to think I had resilience and grit built in from a young age. Many people assumed I'd left my marriage on account of my success, but it was really the opposite of that! I became successful to support my family.

If there's one thing I could instill in others it would be to keep their faith and stay true to themselves. I encourage others to walk away from situations where they are not valued. I saw my parents go through that when they parted from that church. They may have been turned against, but they never turned against God.

I continue to raise my family with faith and spirituality as our most important values. I try to show my children that they are an example of God's love, and with him, anything they set their hearts to can be achieved.

You Are Enough

Darla Bonk

Darla Bonk is the Founder of Darla Bonk Consulting. She is a compassionate leader and experienced business consultant dedicated to equipping entrepreneurs to fall in love with their businesses again.

As a young executive, Darla was thrown head-first into establishing, developing, and flourishing an all-new division totally from scratch within a Fortune 500. She persevered and consistently led the way in sales, employee retention, and leadership development, generating over $50M in revenue for the company.

Her more than 20 years of corporate, executive, and nonprofit experience has made her a "Leader's Leader."

Darla currently serves on the Fort Myers City Council and in 2023 she founded Darla Bonk Consulting, a natural next step in her life-long dedication to leading and uplifting others. She is also the founder and host of the "On Your Way" podcast.

An Elite Member of KNOW Women Global, Darla was recently honored as one of the 40 OVER 40 women to know in the United States. She was also named a finalist for the 2023 Women in Business APEX awards.

Darla resides in Fort Myers, Fla., where she and her husband run Architectural Metal Flashings, and are actively involved with their community, supporting organizations, and participating in mission work all over the world.

They have four children in their twenties and three fur babies. They love to travel and explore the world together, whether it's a faraway getaway or a quick RV road trip.

"Love people, and you serve them well," Darla says, "In that, you'll find the heart of a leader."

***

"It's never too late to become who you want to be. You have the strength within to start over."

~ F. Scott Fitzgerald

Fleeing an abusive marriage with an eight- and five-year-old in the middle of the night from Tennessee to Florida with a police escort was never part of the plan.

I had to give up a lucrative and successful corporate job, which I *loved*. I cashed in my 401k, loaded up the car in a hurry with whatever items I could, and headed back to a state I never thought I would live in again.

I had to start all over again.

Up until that point, I believed I could make anything work. I could be the glue. I could sacrifice for everyone else. I knew how to compartmentalize. It was how I operated. It was how I could "handle" things.

I had been a successful athlete and student in high school. I sang in choir and in church. I had a full-ride vocal scholarship to college. I graduated college magna cum laude with a degree in communication in six semesters with a son under six months old.

I could accomplish anything I put my mind to, and I knew I could make anything work.

Or so I thought.

What I didn't realize was that "making it work" in a life in which I was merely surviving was no life at all.

I had become a shell of a human being.

I had sacrificed everything I was for someone else and didn't know who I was or who I had become. I realized that life just wasn't going to turn out the way I thought it was, no matter how hard I tried.

Everything I had built was gone. Just gone.

The unique details of the story need not be dissected. Regardless of the volatility of the relationship, I was crushed, heartbroken, and found myself wandering.

The commonality of it all is that we all have parts of our lives we wish could have turned out differently or didn't turn out the way we had hoped, right?

Isn't that just how life is? Something always happens to throw us off our game.

We get setbacks. They stop us dead in our tracks. It paralyzed me.

I questioned everything... *Why didn't he love me? Why wasn't I good enough? What didn't I do right? What did I do wrong? How did we end up here?*

The divorce left me devastated—even though I was grateful to now be safe. I was just devastated.

I had never failed at anything in my life, but I had allowed this situation to allow me to question *everything* I knew about myself to be true.

I questioned *God. Where was He? How did he allow this to happen to me? Why didn't He protect me? Why? Why? Why?*

I never lost my faith, but I surely questioned *everything* about *everything*. I couldn't function. As a single mom, there were years when I did not show up all the way for my kids like I should have because I was too busy feeling sorry for myself. They suffered tremendously as a result.

One day I woke up and I decided: *ENOUGH! If I don't make changes and keep fighting as hard to build a new life as I did to get out of a volatile life, then what was the point?*

So, I decided to get back in the arena.

I could turn this setback into a *set-UP.*

I began to say this over and over to myself: *I am more than this. I am better than the life I had. I am worthy of love. I AM ENOUGH!*

It didn't matter what help books I read. It didn't matter what people tried to tell me to cheer me up. It didn't matter how much other people loved me.

Nothing mattered until I could believe it for myself. I had to love myself before I could ask anyone else to love me. I had to give myself grace. I had to realize that I had to be completely whole on my own.

I began to claw my way back. I began to understand the power of what it truly meant to *know* and *understand* who I am in Christ and whose child I really am.

I grew up in a pastor's home with parents who adored me and always spoke positively about my life. I just didn't know how to accept that positivity because I didn't believe I was worthy of the love they gave me, or the love God was trying to impart to me.

I could sit there and feel sorry for myself, or I could begin to believe what I had been telling myself: *I am worthy.*

I had been very successful in corporate America, and I could do it again.

The mind is so powerful—negatively and positively. We believe the lies we tell ourselves. I had to overcome the lies and doubts I had been telling myself for so long and speak life over me, believe it, and now I had to act on it. I went from a single mom working two or three jobs at times to leading leaders and running two successful businesses.

Today, as a recovering bad-decision-maker and self-doubter, I can now say the greatest gift I have ever given myself aside from choosing Jesus Christ to lead my life is to choose to love myself, get whole, and overcome my limiting beliefs.

Today, I can identify the self-sabotaging thoughts that, had I allowed them to, could have overtaken and controlled my emotions and actions. I know I have the power to choose a different outcome. I get the privilege of living this life, and no one can live it for me.

Now, more than 15 years after that horrific night in January of 2007, I am happily married, my kids are grown and thriving, and I am so thankful for this life.

I get to run our family business with my husband, whom I adore. I have the joy of running my own management consulting firm where I equip owners and entrepreneurs to fall back in love with their businesses and I get to serve this community as a city councilperson as a small token of my thanks for the haven it provided to me when I needed it most.

God is faithful. He has allowed my husband and me to lead other couples in prioritizing marriage, date each other, and love their marriages—it's a gift!

Digging out of the darkness is *the* hardest thing I've ever done in my entire life.

If you are reading this, without a doubt you might be searching for a magic bullet. You might be searching for an *aha* moment. I pray you find that in the pages of this book.

I could keep telling you my story, but I would much rather encourage you with these final words remaining in my chapter.

1. You are enough.
2. You have everything within you right now, today, to accomplish everything you have ever wanted. You might need help to bring it to fruition, but you've got this!
3. You were created and designed as a masterpiece. You have unique abilities and gifts that you and only you can bring to the world for those who need to hear it. Embrace it!
4. You are a good wife. You are a good mother. YES. YOU. ARE! You will be if you haven't found that person yet.
5. You are a good friend, daughter, sister, aunt, niece, etc. Yes. You. Are.
6. You are forgiven. So, forgive yourself.
7. No one can live your life for you but you. So, live it to the fullest!
8. Seek advice but trust yourself. Trust your gut and your instincts!
9. God loves you so much! You are His!
10. Do not let that dream die. It doesn't matter if you are 25 or 55. Don't let it die. Don't just chase your dreams. GO CATCH THEM!
11. Be comfortable being alone. Spend time alone. Go on a trip by yourself. Go treat yourself to dinner. Go see a movie alone. Become comfortable in your own skin.
12. KNOW yourself. LOVE yourself. LIKE yourself.
13. Trust God in all things—not some things. ALL things.
14. Let the past go. Learn from it. You aren't that person anymore, so let it go.

15. Smile. Every day. Smile. Find something to smile about and be grateful for each day.

Instead of shame and dishonor,
you will enjoy a double share of honor.
You will possess a double portion of prosperity in your land,
and everlasting joy will be yours.

~ Isaiah 61:7

Embracing Life's Duality: Grief and Success

Sofia Gonzalez

Sofia L. Gonzalez is the principal partner and chief creative officer of Affluence Media Agency. Sofia helps established professional service brands elevate their passion and create a profitable brand that people know, love, and trust through high-end branding, sales-ready website design, and marketing implementation.

Her knowledge and expertise have not gone unnoticed. She has been honored with awards such as the *Gulfshore Business Magazine* 40 Under 40 Award (2022) and the *Business Observer* 40 Under 40 Award (2023) for her impact in the community in various capacities. Sofia is highly sought after for her expert knowledge in branding and marketing strategy; she speaks on stages sharing her insight with entrepreneurs who are looking to scale their impact in their industry and want to leave a legacy. Recently she spoke at First Ladies Forum & Economic Development Summit in Dubai where she spoke on "How to Create a Luxury Personal Brand that Leads to Legacy." She is also a 7x best-selling and 3x hot new release author on Amazon for her co-authorship of *RISE UP: Women Who Lead Building Legacy.*

***

Life... it's a wild roller coaster, isn't it? Full of those unexpected ups and downs?

It's not just about surviving the ride; it's about how you navigate it that truly counts. To me, that's the beautiful and complex duality of existence. It's about appreciating everything—not just the highs and lows but everything in between.

Let me take you back to last year, a year that undoubtedly stands as one of the toughest I've ever faced. I'd heard the phrase "hitting rock bottom" before, but it was just words until I found myself there, living it. It was as if my entire world had been turned upside down by a single, earth-shattering phone call. "Daddy is *what? Where?*" The pain that surged through me at that moment felt like someone was ripping my heart right out of my chest. I was in disbelief as I tried to find my keys, desperate to rush to the hospital. You see, my dad had a history of health scares, so while I'd received calls like this before, I never once thought that this time would be the last. We said our final goodbyes.

There I was, standing on the edge of despair, trying to come to terms with my father's passing. But in the midst of it all, life was offering opportunities. At the age of 32, I was a co-owner of Affluence Media Agency, a thriving growth inbound marketing agency. Right at that moment, I was on the verge of achieving some remarkable milestones that would define my journey of embracing life's duality.

Just before this, I had achieved something incredible: I became a seven-time best-selling author with a three-time Hot New Release on Amazon for my co-authorship of *RISE UP: Women Who Lead Building Legacy.* This led to me to an opportunity to speak at the First Ladies Forum Economic Development Summit in Dubai. My family was so proud of me, especially my parents. My father always encouraged me to go after everything God has for me. However, the First Ladies Forum Economic Development Summit Dubai was scheduled to happen five days after my father passed. I was conflicted, but deep down, I knew my father would have wanted me to go. I wanted to make him proud.

I found myself torn between conflicting emotions. A whirlwind of thoughts raced through my mind. What would people think if I left for another country so soon after his passing? How could I possibly leave my family, especially my grieving mother, during such a challenging time? These questions kept me awake at night, wrestling with the decision.

Deep down, though, there was an unwavering conviction within me. I knew, beyond any doubt, that my father would have wanted me to seize this opportunity. He had always encouraged me to reach for the stars, to make the most of my potential. In his memory, I chose to honor his legacy by pursuing this journey to Dubai, hoping to make him proud in the process.

So, I went. I stepped onto that stage in Dubai, reflecting on the incredible journey I had been on. Life has taught me that even in the darkest moments, there's a glimmer of hope, a chance to rise above adversity.

My choice to attend the event proved to be pivotal. It afforded me the chance to meet remarkable women who were effecting tangible change within their respective countries. I found myself standing before businesses, governments, and organizations from across the globe, all gathered in one forum to deliberate and recommend solutions for enhancing their diverse communities. It was a remarkable opportunity. I also had the privilege of joining my fellow authors on our global book tour, where I shared my insights, both in my chapter titled "Depression Masked as Happiness" and in a talk titled "How to Create a Luxury Personal Brand that Leads to Legacy."

Then just when I thought life couldn't throw any more surprises my way, fate had another twist in store for me. I received the incredible honor of being recognized as part of the prestigious "40 Under 40" by *Gulfshore Business Magazine* and Wink News.

Life's adversities can either break you down or provide the chance for a transformation; for this story, I experienced both. The passing of my father tore me apart emotionally, but it also became the catalyst for a transformation I never could have predicted.

In the midst of my grief, I felt like a butterfly emerging from its cocoon. My father's passing forced me to shed my old self and embrace a new identity. It was a journey that required me to become stronger and more determined. I felt surrounded by a network of prayer warriors, my loving family, the support of my church community, dear friends, and a newfound sense of purpose.

I couldn't remain at the bottom; I had responsibilities to uphold and dreams to chase. I had a company to run, clients who depended on me, a family that needed emotional support, and self-care that I couldn't neglect. So, I made a conscious effort to get back on track with my self-care and healing journey.

My daily routine became my lifeline. I dedicated early mornings to prayer and meditation, followed by a rigorous 6 a.m. boot camp. I recited daily affirmations to keep my spirits high, delved into client work, and squeezed in a second workout. I purged negative thoughts, patterns, people, and clutter from my life that were no longer serving me (literally making space for God to enter and fill those voids). Evenings were dedicated to more affirmations, reinforcing my determination to rise above life's challenges.

One of the challenges and blessings I inherited from my dad is The Hive Community Development Corporation. It's a faith-based community organization that's been active since 2017. The Hive CDC is an asset-based community development corporation with a mission to drive economic development and improve the quality of life in SWFL. We're here to boost the local economy, nurture business incubation, and empower SWFL. From supporting the arts to promoting affordable housing and education, we're dedicated to helping families. What excites me the most is our plan to build a technology center.

Sounds like I have a lot on my plate, right? My dad was a true community leader—smart, always looking out for others. He left some big shoes to fill. But it's not just a legacy for me; it's a legacy for the entire community. Honestly, I never thought I'd find myself in this position, but I'm fully committed to carrying on his work. I understand that it's not just about me; it's about making a positive impact on families for generations to come. So, before I dive headfirst into continuing this mission for SWFL, I'm taking some time to heal and prepare for the exciting journey ahead.

Amidst it all, I've had another unexpected honor of receiving the prestigious *Business Observer* 40 Under 40 Award (2023). It's a recognition that has left me honored and filled with gratitude. Out of 271 remarkable individuals nominated from nine counties across Florida, I was chosen as one of the standout honorees. To receive such an accolade not once but twice, back-to-back, is a testament to God's grace and favor, and I can't help but acknowledge the divine hand at work in my life.

Fast forward to today, and I find myself in Hawaii, taking a much-needed pause for the next six months.

Sitting in serene beauty, I'm hard at work on a book that aims to be a guiding light for those embarking on their own healing journeys. But I'm not just here to write a book; this is a time to reignite my passion projects, those dreams that lingered in the background while I was building my business.

This rest stop is an opportunity for me to climb to the metaphorical mountaintop and receive those divine downloads as I step into the new chapter of healing and wholeness.

One of those dreams, a secret I'm about to spill, is all about modeling. Yes, you heard it right! I'm talking about strutting my stuff on the runway right here in Hawaii. Who would've thought, right? For years, I let the fear of what others might think or say hold me back. I allowed self-doubt to convince me I wasn't good enough. But after the loss of my father, there are no words or thoughts that can hurt me more than losing him. So here I am, living that dream and, let me tell you, it feels absolutely incredible. I've even learned "The Dior Turn." I'm owning that runway and taking a leap into the very things I've daydreamed about for years. So, *shhh...* this is our little secret, and it's just the beginning of something absolutely amazing!

As I soak in the serene beauty of these island landscapes, I can't help but draw parallels between the Hawaiian scenery and the twists and turns of my own life. It's like Hawaii itself, with its mix of peaceful beaches and rugged volcanic terrain, mirroring the ebb and flow of my journey. My life, much like this landscape, has seen moments of quiet introspection and hurdles that required sheer determination.

Life has a remarkable way of revealing its dual nature—the constant interplay of grief and success. It's a bit like a rollercoaster ride, full of unexpected twists and turns. It teaches us to appreciate the intricate balance of life, where grief and joy, loss and success, heartache and hope coexist.

As my journey unfolds, I hope my story can serve as an inspiration for you to embark on your own voyage of self-discovery. I encourage you to embrace the unique duality of your own life. We are not solely defined by our hardships, nor are we confined by our triumphs. It's the harmonious blend of these experiences that empowers us to shape a legacy, one that reflects the indomitable spirit that resides within each of us.

I've come to realize that it's often in our darkest moments that we find the inner strength to shine the brightest. After all, it's within the tapestry of life's duality that we truly discover our authentic selves and the boundless potential that lies within us.

Navigating the intricate duality of life, where grief and success coexist, can indeed be a challenging endeavor. Drawing from my own journey, I've discovered solace and strength in Christian practices that have been a guiding light through the highs and lows.

Here, I share four ways that may help you navigate life's duality:

1. **Prayer and Meditation:** Begin your day with prayer, a powerful avenue to connect with God and find inner peace during turbulent times. Spend moments in conversation

with Him, sharing your burdens and seeking His guidance. Meditation, too, holds great value. It allows you to quiet your mind, attune yourself to God's whispers, and gain clarity amidst chaos. Often, it's in these quiet moments of communion with God that you receive the strength to endure and the wisdom to move forward.

2. **Gratitude Journaling:** Amidst grief and challenges, it's easy to overlook the blessings that still surround us. Maintaining a gratitude journal is a wonderful practice. Each day, jot down the things you're thankful for, no matter how small they may seem. This practice redirects your focus from despair to gratitude, reminding you of God's constant presence and love.

3. **Community and Fellowship:** Remember, you don't have to walk this journey alone. Reach out to your family and friends for support. Share your burdens with them, and allow them to pray for you. Often, the power of collective prayer can offer comfort and strength beyond measure.

4. **Scripture Study and Reflection:** The Bible serves as a timeless source of wisdom and comfort. During times of duality, turn to the Scriptures for guidance and reflection. Seek out passages that resonate with your experiences and meditate on their meanings. God's word possesses a unique ability to provide peace, direction, and inspiration.

The duality of life offers a unique blend of challenges and growth opportunities. Integrating these Christian practices into your daily routine can help you navigate life's highs and lows with unwavering faith and resilience. I'm also on a journey, curating *The Healed Babe*, a book aimed at providing additional guidance and inspiration for your personal healing journey. Together, we can find strength and healing as we embrace life's duality and discover the power within us to overcome.

If you're eager to continue this journey of healing with me and seek further insights on navigating life's duality, I wholeheartedly invite you to stay connected. Follow my ongoing progress as I curate *The Healed Babe*, and join me on this transformative path. Together, we can uncover healing, purpose, and the inner strength needed to rise above life's challenges.

Keep an eye out for updates, and let's walk hand in hand on this healing journey. You can follow me at @thehealedbabe, @elevateyourpassion, and @affluencemedia. Use the hashtags #TheHealedBabe, #ThePassionistaNetwork, and #AffluenceMediaAgency to connect with our community and stay inspired.

AGAINST ALL ODDS

Dayra "Dee" Dominguez

Dayra "Dee" Dominguez is a remarkable individual known for her exceptional creativity, intelligence, and friendly demeanor. Born with a natural inclination towards helping others, Dee has always strived to make a positive impact on the lives of those around her. From a young age, Dee displayed an insatiable curiosity and an eagerness to learn. This led her to pursue higher education, where she excelled academically and gained valuable knowledge in various fields. Her passion for the field of nursing and caregiving allowed her to become a well-rounded individual, capable of approaching any challenge with a creative and analytical mindset.

Dee's friendly and empathetic nature has also played a significant role in shaping her character. Whether it's lending a listening ear to a friend in need or offering guidance to those seeking advice, Dee consistently demonstrates a genuine desire to support and uplift others. Her ability to connect with people on a deep level has made her a trusted confidante and a source of inspiration for many. Furthermore, Dee's creative talents shine through her various endeavors. Her innovative ideas and problem-solving skills have enabled her to tackle complex projects and find unique solutions. Whether it's within the realm of nursing, networking, volunteering in the community, or business, Dee's knack for thinking outside the box and her attention to detail has set her apart from the crowd.

In addition to her intellectual pursuits, Dee is an advocate for personal growth and self-improvement. She firmly believes in the power of continuous learning and strives to expand her skills and knowledge in various areas. Her commitment to personal development not only benefits her but also allows her to better assist and inspire those she interacts with. In conclusion, Dayra "Dee" Dominguez is a friendly, creative, and smart individual who possesses a remarkable ability to help others. With her exceptional intellect, unwavering kindness, and innovative thinking, Dee continues to make a positive impact on the lives of those fortunate enough to know her.

***

"In this life, you will have some trials and tribulations. You cannot allow what happens to you to dictate who and what you become. Make a decision to do better and be better." - Bobby F. Kimbrough Jr.

My name is Dayra Estella Dominguez, but most people call me "Dee." My story began in the summer of 1979.

What's so interesting about my life? The truth is that I don't know. I am sharing my story because I wish someone had shared their story with me earlier in life. I feel like if this had happened, the road may have been less painful and less bumpy.

I became pregnant at 15. My mother was disappointed because she wanted better for me. She did not want me to have the same outcome as her. She, too, had been a teen mother—at seventeen—and was a single mother living in government-subsidized housing. Growing up on public assistance with a single mother presented numerous hardships and challenges. The struggle to make ends meet on a limited income created a constant atmosphere of financial insecurity. The stress of not having enough money for necessities—food, clothing, and shelter—always weighed heavily on my mother, as well as my siblings and me. There was much anxiety and uncertainty in our household as we struggled to just survive.

Growing up in public assistance often meant living in neighborhoods with limited resources and opportunities. Access to quality education, healthcare, and extracurricular activities was minimal, and this further exacerbated the disadvantages my family faced. The lack of access to these fundamental resources hindered our development and future prospects, which made it difficult to break the cycle of poverty and increased our chances of becoming a "statistic."

Moreover, the absence of a second parental figure created emotional and psychological challenges. My mother carried the weight of providing emotional support and stability for us to the best of her abilities all while dealing with her stress and struggles. While we yearned for belonging and guidance from a father figure, we were all doing our best. So, imagine my mindset knowing all of this, having lived this, and possibly having my own child go through this.

I faced immense challenges when I became a teen parent. My husband and I had a tough road in front of us. Despite the overwhelming obstacles, I was determined to demonstrate strength and resilience and overcome any hardships that came my way. In the face of societal judgment and criticism, I refused to let negativity define me. Instead, I focused on my responsibilities as a parent and my love for my child. I sought support from my loved ones but found myself alone during this challenging time. My determination to provide a bright future for my child fueled my motivation to succeed.

I understood that education was crucial in breaking the cycle of adversity. But it was not immediate. By 17, I had obtained my GED, but I was also pregnant for the second time! Despite the demands of being a young parent, I diligently pursued several jobs, ensuring that my children would have all they needed. We wanted "The American Dream" for our children. Recognizing the importance of financial stability, my husband displayed a remarkable work ethic, taking on multiple jobs and embracing the responsibility of being a provider.

Our unwavering commitment to creating a secure and nurturing environment for our children drove our relentless pursuit of success. Throughout my journey, I almost lost sight of my dreams. I remained focused on personal growth and self-improvement, constantly seeking opportunities to develop new skills and expand my knowledge. My determination to create a better life for myself and my family always reminds me that no obstacle is insurmountable. My entire life was dedicated to my children and my husband. For the next 20 years, all I would do was make sure their lives were totally different from mine, far from government-subsidized housing, poverty, and all the negativity that comes from that world.

Now, please do not misunderstand me: I am not ashamed of where I came from for that was what shaped me to be who I am today. However, I wanted something different for my children. I lost part of myself during those years. I knew that I was meant for something more than raising my children, I just didn't know what that was.

At 35, I was diagnosed with low-grade endometrial stromal sarcoma, a sporadic uterine cancer. Needless to say, my life was turned upside down. For the first time in my life, I feared death. How can I leave my children? They still needed me! I got on my knees and asked God to cure me and allow me to remain here for my family. I made a promise to God himself! I told God I would walk in HIS purpose if he cured my cancer. My life was in his hands now, and he did it! He healed me; now it was up to me to do my part of the deal.

The problem was that I needed to learn what HIS purpose for me was. All I knew was being a mom and a wife. I had no other "skills." I had worked as a table games dealer in casinos, a waitress, a bartender, a health educator, and a certified nurse's assistant. I had always cared for people, but I didn't realize at the time I could turn that into a valuable skill.

I took prerequisite nursing classes here and there, but never seriously focused on my education after getting my GED.

At 38, when my youngest was ready to start high school, I made the decision to go back to school! I was already a grandmother and felt like I had not accomplished anything significant in life. You see, for me (at that time), raising my kids and dedicating my life to them and my family was just what I was supposed to do. Many women (especially in Hispanic cultures) take the importance of being a present figure in our children's lives for granted.

I decided to figure out what my "purpose" was. I knew everything I had lived, experienced, and survived was for a bigger purpose! I enrolled in nursing school and graduated (with honors) at 40 years old! The first thing I did was go visit the school where I received my GED (it was a special teen mothers' program). God put in my heart to make a visit and to let the young ladies in that school know that there is a light at the end of the tunnel. The day I walked out of that school, I knew I would continue to be an example for teen mothers in our community.

My story was about changing narratives, so I founded "Against All Odds International." I wanted to become the person I wished I had in my corner when I was 15. My journey would've been different if I had had someone to guide and mentor me. Our past experiences can serve as valuable lessons and catalysts for personal growth, no matter how challenging or complex.

Instead of dwelling on regrets, I use my past as a stepping stone toward a better future. I have learned from my mistakes, embraced the lessons learned, and used them as fuel to drive positive change in my life. By understanding the impact of my past choices and experiences, I can make more informed decisions and take proactive steps toward achieving my goals. Rather than letting regret hold me back, I am determined to harness the wisdom gained from my past to shape a brighter and more fulfilling future.

Against All Odds International (501c3) focuses on helping teen parents overcome obstacles faced in today's society. I want these young men and women to know that even though they became parents at a very young age, they, too, can accomplish their dreams. I will not sugarcoat anything, and I pride myself on sharing my story transparently. My wish is for them to learn and benefit from my mistakes. As a leader in my community and with God by my side, I will continue to overcome any obstacle in my life, and I will continue to Slay in SWFL and the rest of the world!

I hope my journey as a teen parent showcases my incredible strength, resilience, and unwavering determination. Overcoming societal judgment, pursuing education, seeking employment, and never losing sight of my dreams, by the grace of God, I was able to rise above the challenges I faced. I also hope that my story inspires others, proving that with perseverance and a positive mindset, one can triumph over adversity and create a bright future.

As a loving mother, devoted wife, and proud grandmother, one of my deepest desires is for my family to feel a sense of pride in my accomplishments. I strive to be a positive role model for my children, showing them the importance of hard work, perseverance, and pursuing one's passions. I want to instill in them the belief that anything is possible with dedication and determination. By achieving my goals and making a meaningful impact in the world, I aim to inspire my loved ones to dream big and chase their aspirations. Ultimately, the greatest joy for me would be knowing that my children, husband, and grandchildren are proud of the person I have become and the legacy I leave behind.

With love,

Dayra "Dee" Dominguez R.N.

WHAT IF I TOLD YOU YOU'VE GOT WHAT IT TAKES? WOULD YOU BELIEVE ME?

Sylvia Dorisme

Sylvia K. Dorisme is a multifaceted professional, a school owner, savvy entrepreneur, and speaker whose journey exemplifies resilience and the unwavering determination to inspire future generations. As the president and founder of Zeal Technical Institute, Sylvia's life story is a testament to the triumph of the human spirit.

Sylvia's early years were marked by formidable challenges that would have deterred most. Yet, she not only persevered but thrived emotionally and professionally. Her Haitian-American immigrant background as an unaccompanied minor fueled her dreams of breaking barriers in her family. Today, she stands as a beacon of success, firmly in control of her destiny, with a profound commitment to improving the lives of those around her.

Although she may argue that her entrepreneurship journey started at the age of nine, at the age of 25, after facing job loss, she channeled the entrepreneurial spirit instilled in her by her grandmother—to establish Zeal Technical Institute. Over the past 14 years, the institute has grown, offering a range of healthcare programs approved by the Florida Department of Education. The institute has had over 6,000 graduates since its inception. Through marriage, a painful divorce, custody battles, business challenges, family challenges, brokenness, childhood traumas, and heartbreaks, while raising her son as a single mother, she perseveres and continues to thrive.

Sylvia K. Dorisme's story serves as a profound inspiration to all, reminding us that with determination and a commitment to community and self, one can overcome adversity and achieve remarkable success.

***

Growing up in three different countries as a child was a unique and challenging experience that left a lasting impact. As I navigated the unfamiliar cultural landscapes and tried to understand the world around me, each transition brought a wave of confusion. From the language spoken at home to the food on our table, everything seemed to change overnight. I felt like a puzzle piece trying to fit into three different puzzles, never quite belonging anywhere.

These constant moves took a toll on my emotional well-being. I found myself traumatized by the frequent uprooting and the struggle to establish a sense of belonging. Making friends only to leave them behind was heart-wrenching, and I often felt like an outsider looking in on the lives of others. The trauma of these childhood experiences and the unspoken cultural traumas experienced at home left scars that I carry with me to this day.

My early life was marked by a truly unique and challenging situation: my mother, at the tender age of 15, took on the responsibilities of marriage and motherhood. It was clear that she was not fully prepared for the immense demands and complexities that came with parenting at such a young age. This lack of readiness to be a parent meant that my grandmother played a pivotal role in raising me.

My grandmother became my guiding light, stepping into the role of caregiver and mentor. She was the source of most of my foundational principles and values. Her teachings emphasized qualities like love, responsibility, resilience, and the importance of a strong work ethic. It was through her wisdom and unwavering support that I learned to navigate the world and shape my character. My grandmother, to whom I owe a wealth of gratitude, will always be one of my "whys."

While my mother may not have been prepared for the rigors of parenthood at such a young age, I want to express my heartfelt gratitude for her efforts. She faced the challenging journey of early marriage and motherhood with determination and commitment, and her sacrifices did not go unnoticed. Her love and dedication to providing for our family, despite her own youth, are worthy of recognition and appreciation. I can't fathom the mental capacity and emotional strength to navigate family and marriage at such an early age.

My parents' decision to send me away at an early age was rooted in their own traumatic experiences as a young married couple. To them, it may have seemed like a necessary choice, but its impact on me was profound. Separation during my formative years left me with a deep sense of longing and a hunger for connection. Yet, through this experience, I learned resilience and independence, gaining a unique perspective on life's challenges. While their decision bore unintended consequences, it also contributed to my personal growth and shaped the person I've become. Throughout my healing journey, I've learned to forgive my parents for sending me to the United States alone at the tender age of 14 to fend for myself.

My journey as an unaccompanied minor to the United States marked a pivotal chapter in my life, fraught with immense challenges that would ultimately shape my character and determination to become an entrepreneur or what I sometimes call a "mompreneur." The process of immigration was a daunting and bewildering experience. Separated from my family, I felt the weight of uncertainty and isolation as I embarked on this solitary path towards an unknown future.

Upon arrival, the challenges only intensified. I found myself trying to find my identity and learning to be responsible at such a young age. During high school, the choice to continue or not was entirely up to me. Shortly after I went through 13 different homes and found out my first real boyfriend cheated on me, I encountered short-term homelessness, struggling to find a place to sleep and a way to sustain myself. The nights were often cold and long, and hunger was a constant companion. I felt like a stranger in a strange land, trying to navigate a complex system with no one to guide me. The feeling of isolation was overwhelming, and at times, it seemed like the world was against me.

Perhaps the most painful aspect of this journey was the alienation from my family. The distance, both physical and emotional, between us grew wider with each passing day. The sense of abandonment and the longing for their presence weighed heavily on my heart. It was a painful realization that I had to forge my path alone, with little support or guidance. A traumatic experience that I've had to find peace with.

But adversity has a way of revealing our inner strength, and at the age of 18, I made a conscious decision to take control of my life. I refused to be defined by my circumstances or let them dictate my future. It was a turning point, a moment when I resolved to never look back. I sought education and employment opportunities, gradually rebuilding my life one step at a time.

This journey has taught me resilience, self-reliance, and the importance of never losing hope. It has shaped my belief that we have the power to overcome even the most daunting obstacles when we refuse to surrender to adversity. While my past is marked by challenges and hardship, it has also instilled in me an unwavering determination to create a better future for myself. Today, I stand as a testament to the strength of the human spirit, driven by the lessons learned through hardship and the unyielding resolve to never give up.

As an entrepreneur with nearly two decades of experience, my journey has been marked by a series of formidable challenges that have tested my resolve and resilience.

I began my entrepreneurial journey with limited capital, armed primarily with passion and a vision. Starting from scratch, I faced financial constraints that made every decision critical. The early years were punctuated by failures, each one a harsh lesson in the unforgiving world of business. These setbacks weighed heavily on my confidence, but I understood that success often emerges from the ashes of failure.

In addition to professional setbacks, I grappled with personal challenges. A failed romantic relationship left emotional scars that

I carried into my entrepreneurial endeavors. The joy of becoming a new mom was clouded by postpartum depression, adding a layer of complexity to an already demanding life. A challenging divorce further complicated matters, with the legal and emotional toll it exacted.

Navigating the turbulent waters of business as a single mom was perhaps one of the most daunting tasks I faced. Balancing the responsibilities of parenthood with the demands of entrepreneurship was a constant struggle. Simultaneously, I found myself embroiled in a custody battle, a draining experience that tested my emotional endurance.

Amid these challenges, I ventured into new business opportunities, some of which resulted in failed ventures. Private battles and personal hardships added weight to my already full plate. The pressures of my community involvement added an additional layer of complexity. It felt like a never winning battle, and there were days I wanted to give up entirely.

It is undeniable that being an entrepreneur, especially as a woman determined to succeed, is a formidable undertaking. The path is fraught with obstacles that can at times seem insurmountable. However, I firmly believe that while it may not be easy, it is indeed possible to overcome these challenges.

Taking responsibility for oneself is paramount. It entails acknowledging that setbacks are not synonymous with failure; rather, they are stepping stones to growth. An open mind is indispensable, allowing for adaptation and learning from mistakes. Trusting in God and the process provides solace, reminding us that we do not have to bear the weight of the world on our shoulders.

Being a woman who excels in the entrepreneurial world is undoubtedly a challenge, but it is a challenge that can be conquered with resilience, determination, and an unwavering belief in the journey, no matter how arduous it may be. The difficulties faced along the way are opportunities for growth and transformation, and I continue to press forward with the knowledge that the path may be tough, but the destination is worth every effort.

However, amidst the confusion and trauma, I learned three valuable lessons that have guided me through life. The first lesson was to accept my situation. I realized that while I couldn't control the circumstances of my upbringing, I could control how I responded to them. Embracing my unique background and experiences allowed me to find strength in my differences.

The second lesson was to design a plan. Instead of allowing circumstances to dictate my path, I began to set goals and work towards them. I recognized that I had the power to shape my own destiny and make choices that aligned with my aspirations. This proactive approach helped me regain a sense of control over my life.

The third and perhaps most important lesson was to never give up. I refused to let the challenges and setbacks define me. I learned to persevere through adversity, knowing that every obstacle was an opportunity for growth. This resilience has been my greatest asset, enabling me to overcome the trauma of my childhood and thrive in the face of adversity.

My journey of being raised in three different countries was marked by confusion, trauma, and the struggle to belong. However, it also taught me valuable lessons in acceptance, planning, and resilience. While the scars of my past remain, they serve as a reminder of the strength I've gained through my unique experiences.

Balancing Ambition and Motherhood

Vanessa M. Chaviano

Vanessa M. Chaviano is a seasoned entrepreneur with over 18 years of marketing and business operations expertise. With a dual bachelor's degree and a master's in Criminal Forensic Studies from Florida Gulf Coast University, she later pursued an MBA in Organizational Leadership from Ashford University. Vanessa was honored as one of Gulfshore Business Magazine's 40 under 40, Women of Distinction Non-Profit Leader Finalist for 2021, Rotary of Cape Coral Rookie of the Year for 2020-2021, Florida Gulf Coast University SBDC Distinguished Entrepreneur Finalist for 2022, Angels Among Us Award, 2022 ENPYs Award Finalist for the Connie Ramos-Williams Nonprofit Publicity Award, 2022 Lideres Award, and nominee for the Women in Business 2023 APEX Awards.

Driven by her commitment to empowering women and nurturing future leaders within the Hispanic community, Vanessa established Leading Latina, a 501c3 non-profit organization. Its primary objective is to advance and promote personal and professional growth among women. As the founder and President, Vanessa works tirelessly to fulfill the organization's mission.

In addition to her entrepreneurial pursuits, Vanessa actively engages in various leadership roles. She is the Director and Public Image Chair for the Rotary Club of Cape Coral, Cape Competes Stakeholder Member, The Hispanic Vote Board of Directors, Leadership Cape Coral 2023 Chair, and the 2022-2023 Cape Coral Chamber of Commerce Board Member.

Vanessa cherishes her role as a wife to her husband, Humberto, and as a loving mother to their two daughters, Sadie, and Olivia.

***

The unexpected question landed like a heavy blow, catching me off guard. My husband and I were seated at the dining table, deep in conversation about a career opportunity that had presented itself. At that time, my workplace was a whirlwind of activity, marked by mergers and acquisitions, and my vice president had floated the idea of exploring opportunities at our Atlanta headquarters.

My career had been a journey marked by perseverance. Transitioning from a role within a car dealership to supporting them as a marketing vendor, I devoted five years to the company, weathering two mergers and rising from an account manager to a supervisor and then a department manager. It was a trailblazing journey that saw me become the first woman to secure a manager position within the organization.

This phase felt like the zenith of my career. I was earning well, residing in the home I had built seven years prior, enjoying excellent benefits, and representing a reputable automotive company. However, the bombshell hit when the company announced another merger, reshuffling the entire organizational structure. It was a seismic shift, leaving me pondering my department's fate and role. In an instant, they vanished.

As I laid out the magnitude of these organizational changes to my partner, I passionately explained how it could impact my career's trajectory. I had dedicated immense effort and made personal sacrifices to reach where I was. A clear path to success had been laid out, but with these changes, everything was uncertain. I felt like the ground had been pulled from beneath my feet, and I was facing a setback of several years. To complicate matters, I was asked to take on a role managing a remote team I had never even met.

Then, out of the blue, my husband posed a question that left me bewildered and frustrated, "So, why did you want to have a child if you wanted to grow your career?" It was a question I hadn't anticipated and had never crossed my mind. I couldn't fathom why I had to choose between the two. Such a question wouldn't arise if the roles were reversed, with a man facing a career decision. I had fought to make a name for myself in a predominantly male-dominated field, and I was finally at the table, making a difference as the only woman in a room full of men.

My husband had never adhered to traditional gender norms or outdated beliefs, and for the majority of our relationship, I had been the primary breadwinner. Our household responsibilities and parenting duties were evenly split, defying conventional roles. Our setup might have appeared unconventional in our Spanish household, with him taking charge of cooking while I managed the cleanup. Despite my ability to cook, he was the culinary maestro, and it was a division that worked for us.

My upbringing had been marked by challenges. Raised in a single-parent household, I saw my mother juggle multiple jobs to provide for my siblings and me. I vividly remembered dinners by candlelight due to power outages and wearing hand-me-down clothes. We couldn't afford name-brand items, and walking to the grocery store was our transportation. These experiences left a lasting impression on me, instilling a fierce determination to achieve financial security. I had contingency plans for every scenario and purchased my house as a symbol of stability and self-reliance.

I was resolute about never experiencing the struggles of my childhood again. My mother did her best with her resources; those formative experiences shaped my personal and professional outlook. I embraced every opportunity that came my way and thrived on adapting to challenges on the fly.

So, when my husband posed that unexpected question, I was taken aback. Why couldn't I have both—a fulfilling career and motherhood? I saw it as pursuing the dream of "having it all," not an unreasonable aspiration. After all, he worked in retail sales, earning a living, but was not particularly passionate about his job. In contrast, I had a promising career in management and was on the path to a director position, leveraging the skills and education I had diligently acquired.

I was effecting change, implementing new processes, and making a tangible impact in my department. Suddenly, because I was a mother, it seemed like my career growth was in jeopardy. That was a notion I had never entertained.

Our conversation was heading nowhere, and the prospect of relocating to Atlanta, which was on the table, would require me to go alone. It would disrupt my husband's time with his older daughter and distance him from family and friends. Moving meant breaking up our family, something I was unwilling to do. I was determined to strike a balance between motherhood and my career.

My unwavering commitment was not just for my benefit but for my daughter's future as well. I had come too far to abandon everything I had worked tirelessly for. Motherhood was a cherished aspect of my life, but I refused to limit myself to a single role. My career represented my security and safety net, and I was unwilling to relinquish it. What I had earned was rightfully mine, regardless of whether others understood my reasoning.

That question had rekindled my childhood struggles, and I vowed to do more and be more for my daughter. When my husband and I first crossed paths, I juggled two jobs to make ends meet. Fresh out of a divorce, I was in a period of healing and self-discovery. While I dated occasionally, those relationships helped me define the qualities I sought in a partner—someone who would allow me to be myself.

As a Hispanic woman, I often challenged stereotypes and embraced a "just watch me" attitude. In the male-dominated automotive industry, women were often relegated to answering phones, scheduling appointments, or working in accounting. The stereotype persisted that intelligence and beauty couldn't coexist. I shared the camaraderie of countless women in the industry who could relate to my experiences. I greatly respected those rare women who broke into finance or management roles.

My ambitious and tenacious nature drove me to prove I could achieve anything I set my mind to. Those words of encouragement from my past had shaped my determination. My unwillingness to play a subordinate role in previous relationships had led to their demise. I was relentlessly hungry for success and perpetual self-improvement.

I possessed the capability to stand on my own, a trait that was both a blessing and a curse. I sought a partner who didn't feel threatened by my ambition and was comfortable with me pursuing my personal and professional goals, whatever they may be.

In my fervor to advocate for myself and my circumstances, I hadn't stepped back and understood why my husband had asked that question. I immediately went into defense mode, erecting walls, and donning armor. It was remarkable how past trauma could influence our reactions and perceptions. Our childhood experiences shape the lens through which we viewed the world.

At that moment, I was upheaving my husband's life at the dining table, asking him to make a profound change and provide an immediate answer. It was an unfair demand, and my irrational response didn't help. Until then, he had supported me through every challenge, from countless late nights at work to week-long business trips when our daughter was just a few months old. His unwavering support was a new dynamic in our relationship, one I wasn't accustomed to yet.

Not only was I attempting to balance motherhood with my career, but I was also learning how to navigate a healthy relationship. My husband's question had acted as a catalyst, forcing me to confront my own expectations and the complexities of our partnership.

In the following weeks, we engaged in numerous heartfelt conversations, exploring the roots of our concerns and aspirations. We unearthed the fears and insecurities that had led to that pivotal question. It was a journey of self-discovery and mutual understanding.

We realized that our partnership was built on a foundation of love and respect, one that allowed us to pursue our individual dreams while supporting each other's growth. We acknowledged the importance of open communication, empathy, and compromise in maintaining a healthy balance between our personal and professional lives.

As we continued to evolve as individuals and as a couple, I found solace in knowing that I didn't have to choose between my career and motherhood. Instead, I could embrace both aspects of my life fully. It was a challenging journey, but it taught me that with the right partner and a willingness to adapt, I could indeed have it all—a thriving career, a fulfilling family life, and a loving relationship.

MARKETING MYSELF... A GAME PLAN TO REPOSITION FEAR, FAILURE, AND FAITH INTO FORGIVENESS

Kendra Sutton

Kendra Sutton is a visionary entrepreneur whose life has been an adventurous tapestry spanning various industries. She has worked in the oil and manufacturing sector, professional sports, the concert and entertainment industry, and television broadcasting. She now owns her own advertising and marketing agency, KD Sutton Creative Solutions, LLC, and she has definitely enjoyed the ride!

Kendra began her professional journey in the oil and manufacturing industry at a young age. Her desire to work in pro sports led her to work for renowned teams in the NHL, IHL, ECHL, and NBA.

Working in various entertainment arenas facilitated her cross-over into the concert and show industry. Her bold move into this exciting world marked the beginning of an incredible 11-year journey. Her work as one of only a few women in sports at the time showcased her professionalism, set the stage for future endeavors, and opened doors for many women in the industry, as well as starting a women's hockey league in Southwest Florida that still exists today.

In 2003, Kendra took the courageous step of establishing a sports consulting and marketing business, traveling the United States to help sports teams. Seeking a more balanced home life, Kendra transitioned into business consulting and advertising sales with Fox Television Network, which then led her to WINK News and the CBS Network, where she spent an impressive 13 years.

In 2020, during a global pandemic and with the sudden task of caregiving for her father, Kendra received a divine call to return to her entrepreneurial roots. This pivotal moment led to her desire to start her own advertising and marketing agency.

With divine guidance and collaborative input from both of her parents, KD Sutton Creative Solutions, LLC was founded in January 2021. Her agency has since flourished, thanks to God's will, as well as her dedication, creativity, relationships, AMAZING clients and commitment to excellence.

Kendra attributes everything to the doors that God has opened for her throughout her journey. With an open heart and the courage to obediently step through the opportunities presented to her, KD Sutton Creative Solutions, LLC remains a shining example of what can be achieved through faith, determination, and an unwavering commitment to one's dreams and family.

Her story is a testament to the power of pursuing one's passions, even in the face of challenges.

***

As the saying goes, "What doesn't kill you makes you stronger."

But what if what doesn't kill you leaves you with deep scars that fester beneath the surface, silently shaping your every move and thought?

For most of my life, that's how I operated, not knowing any better. Growing up, I faced a tumultuous childhood marked by trauma, fear, and abandonment that resulted in a severe lack of self-love, insecurities, and relentless self-sabotage. Yet in my quest for perfectionism and approval from others, I somehow managed to hide it all so well (or so I thought). The objective of pursuing success became my constant companion.

But life has a way of unraveling our facades when we least expect it.

As a child, I learned the art of "marketing" in order to survive— I learned how to *position and sell* my sense of self *for others to find my value.* The severely dysfunctional environment I grew up in was the breeding ground for fear, lack, and scarcity. Fearing that revealing my vulnerability would only invite more pain, I became adept at concealing my emotions, or severely mishandling them.

I truly feel this is where my *creativity and imagination* were born.

This fear became the driving force behind my actions. I escaped the chaos at home by excelling in school, sports, and work. I believed that if I could prove my worth through achievements, I might find a path to breaking generational curses.

The *brand* I wore was one of confidence and ambition, a disguise that masked my inner turmoil.

The world saw a successful, driven individual, while I remained imprisoned within my own insecurities. I had thriving careers in pro sports and television. I had someone in my life I loved deeply, an array of animals I adored, numerous friends, a nice home, and lukewarm faith...

I had achieved all of this while concealing the wounds of my past.

Professionally, I was knocking it out of the park; I was a type-A overachiever who was smart, strong, confident, "in control"... and busy *meeting everyone else's wants and needs*. I looked like I had it all together, but my reality was far different. The monsters of self-doubt, fear, and failure continued to haunt me, even as I achieved more.

It was at the age of 53, after decades of wearing this *product of success*, that my life unraveled.

The catalyst for my downfall showed up at my door: My father.

His health—and life—were in crisis. Despite thinking I'd already forgiven him, when I saw him, all the resentment and anger I held toward him catapulted the lid off that Pandora's Box. Yet, when he needed me, I couldn't turn away. There, my carefully constructed "image" crumbled.

It was at that pivotal moment that I was forced to confront my deeply buried emotions—an unforgiving grudge of abandonment, rejection, and betrayal toward my father and a deeply wounded inner child, as a result.

Until then, I had not realized that he had been the source of much of my childhood trauma which had carried over as choices, reactions, and decisions I'd made throughout my adult life.

As the years of caregiving tallied, I saw how I had inherited his poor choices, learned behaviors, and accumulated baggage. I had never truly forgiven him. It was there God started showing me all my past regrets, mistakes, behaviors, wounds, triggers, and piles of dirty laundry that needed to be removed and renewed.

That clarity revealed that *my values, needs, and wants* deserved a voice.

This came with an exchange. My career ended; I lost my animals and relationship; my finances were pushed to the brink.

I felt as if I were losing everything, including myself.

But GOD.

Amid all this chaos, and with a determination like no other, I chose to end the façade. I chose to start trusting myself, my heart, and my gut. Something shifted within me. Perhaps it was the realization that life is too short to carry the weight of unforgiveness, or the sudden awareness that my facade of success had been nothing more than a fragile shell.

Finding my worthiness and self-love was priority; healing and forgiveness were necessary. Healing the past... I compare it to crawling on your knees on shards of glass on top of hot coals, down what looks like a never-ending road. It is not easy but is required if we are to become our true selves. Forgiveness is a journey, and it often begins with the most difficult person to forgive: ourselves.

My transformation wasn't sudden or easy—but it saved my life. I started by acknowledging and confronting the pain I had buried for so long. As I worked through my own issues, I also began the process of forgiving my father.

Forgiving him, and others, was a gift to myself.

I also found an even deeper empathy for a mother who would never discuss her own past. I began to understand that, as a child of trauma herself, she had done her best. She gave me all of what she did have to give, to make up for not having two parents.

Therapy played a crucial role in my healing process, and I had a lot of it in various forms. I've grasped at every straw presented, cherishing what worked and appreciating the experience even if some didn't. But I refused to give up. I am not embarrassed or ashamed. I've allowed myself to grieve for that lost childhood, for the love I never received, for those who have betrayed and hurt me, and for the internal wounds that had festered as a result for decades.

Flaws and all, knowing that I am perfectly Imperfect, I've also now allowed myself to feel and accept love for the first time in my life, all while giving myself permission to be vulnerable, authentic, and transparent.

This is daunting, difficult, uncomfortable, unfamiliar, and painful at times, but necessary to have freedom, joy, and the happy life we desire. Even if it means losing important things in our lives (in my case, my career, relationship, animals, money...all things I clung to tightly.)

Most importantly, faith and prayer have carried me. They have given me the strength to be accountable. I now do whatever is necessary to create a safe space to explore my emotions, confront my trauma, and develop the tools to become the best version of myself for God's purpose. Through therapy and faith, I've learned that God and self-love are not luxuries, but necessities. To learn that, I had to renew my faith, rewire my thinking, *create a different marketing message,* and *reposition* myself with a game plan of overcoming.

With forgiveness came the opportunity for a fresh start. With a long-term career gone, the end of a relationship, and faced with the prospect of losing my home, a symbol of stability I had clung to for years, I refused to let fear paralyze me any longer. Instead, I channeled my newfound faith in myself and a divinely restored past, to start my own business. It was a leap of faith, a daring step into the unknown, but it was also a testament to my resilience.

As I embarked on my entrepreneurial journey of opening my own Marketing and Advertising Agency, I realized that fear had been the silent saboteur of my past. It had held me back from pursuing my dreams, fully experiencing life and love, as well as reaching my true potential. But now, I was determined to let faith guide my decisions instead.

Faith isn't just about religion; it's about trusting in yourself and the universe. It's about believing that you can overcome obstacles and create a better future for yourself. Hope in what is unseen, but completely possible.

I learned that when you replace fear with faith, incredible opportunities emerge.

Today, I see myself much like a successful marketing campaign:

- I am an ongoing process that adapts to changes.
- I aim to see MY value.
- I create meaningful relationships with people.
- I determine success by having faith in my products and Myself.
- I am achieving a sense of fulfillment, contentment, and alignment with my life's purpose.
- I meet my needs and wants and still have plenty to give others.
- I do not sell myself short.
- I work in, and on, myself.

The journey from self-discovery to self-improvement and, ultimately, self-realization mirrors the strategic steps of marketing, demonstrating that transformation is possible with dedication, strategy, and a clear sense of purpose.

How am I doing, you ask? ...Better Now.

Blessed is she who has believed the Lord would fulfill all of HIS promises to her.

~ Luke 1:45 NIV

One in Five

Marissa Gonzalez

Marissa resides in SWFL where she has lived since leaving New Jersey in 2004. She is now an entrepreneur and wears many hats, one of which is as an international advocate for HIV/AIDS. After her diagnosis, she went on a journey where she found healing and self-love. She now advocates for body positivity, reducing HIV-related stigma, and showing that she is much more than her diagnosis. She's a financial literacy educator and recently has gained interest in helping homeowners learn about their options for going solar. She also has leadership, blogging, and ambassador roles in various HIV organizations.

As an entrepreneur and advocate, Marissa spends much of her time educating individuals in each designated area. She travels to attend conferences and trainings, which have taken her to Honduras, Puerto Rico, California, Texas, DC, Boston, and more. Marissa's goal is to show that she leads the life she desires and is not hindered by her medical diagnosis. She's found a sisterhood of women who understand what she faces as a woman living with HIV, and they support one another through the stigma that still exists in our world today.

Follow her on all social platforms to stay up to date with her work as an advocate and entrepreneur.

***

As women, we face many unique struggles, both internal and external. I wasn't exempt from this, but I did once forget that I didn't need to face the adversities alone.

There's usually a moment in our lives when everything changes and totally shifts our full existence, am I right? Well for me that was in 2016, and it was so big that I'll never forget the day.

But before we dive into that, I am compelled to paint the picture for you of what I believe led to the moment that shifted my very existence.

I was born and raised in Paterson, NJ—if you know anything about this city, it is far from vibrant. In my teenage years, it was apparent that life was a struggle and filled with many hardships, none of which I truly understood at such a young age. I grew up with two older brothers in the wrestling era, so my childhood wasn't all about rainbows, butterflies, or Barbies. At a young age, I was diagnosed with PCOS, something that affects 1 in 10 women. At the age of 11, all I knew this meant was heavy periods, extra weight, and hair on parts of my body that other girls did not have.

The kids around me were cruel. I was teased, bullied, and called all kinds of names. I got into so many fights, all before the age of 14, that my mother put me in Catholic school, hoping the fights would stop. She was right, but unfortunately, she wasn't quite prepared for the expenses that came along with my attendance (or lack thereof), so after two years there I was placed back into public school.

For several reasons, my parents decided to move us to Florida in 2004, which was the end of my freshman year. I was devastated to have been taken away from the only place I knew, despite the negative things I had faced. I did have friends I didn't want to leave and had found a certain comfort and sense of peace in Paterson. But through all this, I didn't have much of a relationship with my siblings—in person, it often felt like *I hate you*. But there was a strong love underneath that popped up if someone tried to mess with your siblings.

When we got to Florida, things didn't really get any better. I was adjusting to a totally new city, and again teased for the things that made me "different." I swore if one more person asked me to say coffee or water again—finding humor in my Jersey accent—I would scream. Eventually, I adjusted. Things got better. I made friends, and started to build a life in SWFL. However, I still felt the deep void I'd had for most of my life. The bullying led me to feel empty; the feeling was heightened by not feeling real love from the men in my life.

This void pushed me to look for love in all the wrong places. I had no sense of self-worth and low self-esteem.

I had always been noticed for my smile and my butt, and I grew up believing that these were the greatest things I had to offer a partner. I would become obsessed with any little bit of attention I would get because I didn't have that love for myself. As a result, I ended up with guys who didn't value me for me—they valued my looks. Sometimes, though, being with these men fulfilled that need for love I had longed for.

Through all this, I had remained a social butterfly. I loved going out with friends and buried myself in work and school. I was the girl who always had two or three commitments and not much time to think or be with myself. I realize now just how toxic that was, and how important it is to truly spend time with ourselves, knowing who we are, understanding what brings us joy, and finding happiness within ourselves.

By 2015, my life was going well, I thought. I had friends who seemed solid, I was dating, I traveled a lot, and I was having fun. I wasn't thinking about the consequences of my actions. I've always been the type to make pretty good decisions, but I wore my heart on my sleeve, so my kindness was often taken advantage of. My insecurities sometimes manifested in not the prettiest of ways and put me in some questionable situations.

My love life had not been as successful as the other parts of my life, but I ended up meeting someone who I got along with well. He seemed worth the time and energy of getting to know. Things grew quickly between us, and after just a few months of dating, we moved in together. (We rationalized this by not having to pay two sets of household bills because we were always together.)

It didn't take long for this relationship to become nothing of what I imagined. Countless lies, cheating, arguing, and more went on for almost a year. I stayed because of his "potential." I swore he'd change, and things would get better, but they never got better.

I finally cut ties. The day that he was coming over to get his belongings was the day that changed everything, On May 26, 2016, I was going to reclaim my life. But as he was on his way to the house to get his belongings, I got a call from my gynecologist's office, stating they had scheduled an emergency appointment, and I needed to come in immediately. Previous to this, I'd been proactive about my health and was never asked to come in after the annual testing. I knew there was a problem. After hours of waiting, worrying, and arguing with my doctor's office to get a clear understanding of what the hell I was about to be told, I was told something I wasn't prepared to hear at the age of 26: "You are HIV positive."

I spun into a deep depression and attempted suicide. At that moment, I knew something needed to change. I began doing the self-work to heal the past—not just the traumas from this relationship but all the ones prior, including childhood. I went to therapy, read books, cried, and wrote letters in an attempt to heal. But my true healing began when I found a sisterhood. I was connected with women who knew the struggles I faced. They were able to not only lend a listening ear but also offer advice from their lived experiences through this shared diagnosis.

I learned that, in life, we need to lean on ourselves to work through past traumatic experiences. But we must also have support, a group of friends who can relate to what you are experiencing and share insight into things you may not have yet experienced.

I learned that to receive true, genuine, and kind love from others, I had to be willing to give that to myself in spades. I had to not only treat others how I wanted to be treated, but treat myself that way as well. There are so many nuances that can impact a woman's mental health, and it's important to address each and every one that comes up to truly be the best versions of ourselves.

I found I had to be willing to take risks to learn what makes me *me*. I had to figure out what I truly enjoy versus things I have no interest in, and intentionally remind myself that it's OK to say "no" to things that do not serve me or protect my peace.

I became the hero of my story by allowing others to share their experience and being committed to growing to be a better version of myself. I read books, watched documentaries, listened to podcasts, and had many thought-provoking conversations that pushed me to grow.

As it turns out, the very thing that almost ended my life is the very thing that gave me life. I often remind myself that things normally perceived as "negative" could actually be guiding me to a better future—it's how I choose to respond that matters. When I control my responses in a mature way, when I am proactive instead of giving in to negative emotions, I become a better version of myself, and I'm more able to help others as well.

BECOMING UNSTOPPABLE

Jennifer Johnson

Jennifer is a multifaceted entrepreneur who is actively involved in her community. She owns True Fashionistas (Florida's largest lifestyle resale store), Cooies Cookies, Pink Farmhouse (an online store), and The Fashionista Life, which encompasses her podcast, blog, motivational speaking, and coaching business for women entrepreneurs. Jennifer is an inspiration to other women business owners as she shows that it is possible to be successful in business while also making a difference and giving back to her community.

***

I grew up on a dairy farm, the second oldest of six siblings. My parents did whatever they could to make sure they took care of all eight of us in the house. I remember them working long, hard hours on the farm so they could put food on the table.

This farm was the foundation of not only who I was but who I was to become. It was what cultivated my true personal core values.

I've been an entrepreneur for over 25 years. Entrepreneurship does not follow a straight line for everyone; for me, it was more of a wave. I started by founding a wedding and event planning business from my home. This evolved into a bridal shop, and eventually a wedding rental business. I founded an online clothing store, and after that, my passions led me to open more businesses: Cooies Cookies, True Fashionistas, and The Fashionista Life.

Throughout my life, every time I found myself aligning with the wrong people, I ended up in some sort of conflict or duress that left me feeling unworthy, not smart enough, not good enough. I'd come out of these situations with much less self-confidence than I had going into them. I realize now that this was because I lacked some fundamentals in really knowing who I was and what I stood for. I didn't know or understand my core values.

Core values are beliefs that guide your life decisions. I like to think of them as guideposts and guardrails—the guideposts light your way, the guardrails keep you from straying off-course. If we can determine what our core values are early on, they can help us cut through all the noise and determine what's truly important to us. I find it helpful to think of them as things that can fill your heart and things that can break your heart. They help you step into your awesomeness in life and help you carry the passion in your heart to live your best life.

We come into this world with core values, and they are revealed to us throughout our lives. Often, they reveal themselves to us in small quiet whispers. Our life is always speaking to us in whispers... we just have to pay attention.

These whispers inspire, motivate, and guide us.

When I was in high school, I started dating a guy who I had worked with. At first, I was reluctant to date him. I'm not sure why, but I was. (There's something to be said about our intuition and gut feelings—always pay attention to them! I now think of these as my "whispers.") We began dating and after about the second or third date, I had already begun seeing signs of control. For example, one evening after a movie, I told him I wanted to go home. He said, "No I won't let you go home, you have to be with me tonight." I was scared and wanted to get out of the car right away. He started fighting with me, and I told him that I never wanted to see him again. He started hitting his steering wheel and told me that if I ever said anything like that again, or if I did leave him, he would kill me. Being so young and naïve, I thought he was just kidding around about the killing part. I thought it was just a figure of speech.

But he wasn't kidding.

This violence continued. He began calling me names and telling me that I was no good, he kept telling me that I was ugly. He told me I was lucky to have him because if I didn't, I would never find anyone to love me. Then the hitting started. At first, I thought he was just playing around and sometimes would get carried away.

Not so.

Once he accused me of cheating on him with his friend (which I hadn't done). In his rage, he threw me against the wall and I almost blacked out. What made me feel even worse and more worthless was that coworkers had watched him do this to me, and they didn't say a word or do anything.

I told my parents and one of my friends about the violence, and they urged me to leave him. They told me that I did not deserve to be treated this way and encouraged me to report the incidents to the police. But I didn't; this was a small town where everyone knew everyone else's business, and I was afraid of being humiliated.

The violence continued. On many occasions, I was forced to have sex, slapped, kicked, hit, and smothered with pillows. After every one of these violent acts, he promised he would never do it again. He would minimize the situation and say that I was asking for it. It was always "my fault." He brainwashed me in such a way that I began believing everything he was telling me. I stayed in the relationship because I didn't think that I could do any better, and I thought he was going to hurt me and my family. I also thought I could change him.

I earned a college scholarship for a degree in broadcast journalism—this was my dream, and still is to this day. But I ended up not going because he told me if I went, he would kill me and my family as well.

So, as you can imagine, my dreams of being that TV news anchor went out the door.

The final straw came when he knocked me down on the ice in a parking lot in front of his friends. Up until this point, none of his friends had believed me. They thought it was all in my head. Finally, they saw what was happening with their own eyes—yet continued to take his side.

Finally, I told him I never wanted to see him again. I thought it was over, but it wasn't; he stalked me for months after our breakup. He would follow me home after work and try to drive me off the road. On one occasion, he forced me off the road to rape me. He would also call me at all hours of the night to make sure that I was home and not out with anyone else.

I decided that the only way I was going to get out of this situation was to move away.

The last contact that I had with him was about a year later at a town festival. He saw me with my then-boyfriend (now husband), and he began calling me names. He said that he was going to follow us and kill us both. This scared me to death. The next day, I filed an order for protection and received a court date. I was assured these kinds of guys never show up for the court hearing, but he showed up. I was able to get the order for protection, and the nightmare was finally over.

In this entire situation, I lost myself. I lost the sense of who I was. *I lost me.* I didn't realize at the time how much I was giving up to one person who treated me so poorly. The scars I gained during this trying time in my life didn't reveal themselves to me for a very long time—but when they did, they were frightening and unsettling. My fear of water (to this day I still cannot swim with my children) and my claustrophobia (from being smothered) can be so bad at times I can't even wear tight clothing. I have been known to try something on at home and literally cut it off if it felt too constraining.

My point in re-living this story for you is to illustrate how, at that early stage of life, I was so young and naïve and had no idea what I stood for. I had no idea what my core values were, so how in the world could I possibly show that to others? How could other people know what I stood for? How could I surround myself with people who understood what I believed when I didn't even know this myself?

In a way, my past prepared me somewhat for a situation I was to find myself in on my entrepreneurial journey.

When I started True Fashionistas, I didn't have the money to start because I still owned a business in Minnesota and was waiting for it to sell. I had the knowledge to start a business but not the money. A "trusted" friend was willing to provide the money and we would be 50/50 partners. Somehow a few months into the business, she decided she didn't want to do business with me anymore, and we were left with the choice to buy her out or give her the business. We chose to buy her out. The very next day she signed a lease on a store a few doors down from mine, and it was the exact same type of business. To top it off, she took all my employees except for one.

But I didn't let it stop me.

There are so many things that can challenge us in life. Whether a challenge is personal, work, or business, when we know what we stand for (our core values), this can guide us when we need to make important life decisions. Our core values provide us with a roadmap to follow when we reach that fork in the road, that pivotal point where we need to finally take a stand. Knowing our core values can help us to stay on our paths and not be distracted by whatever shiny new object or relationship may be in our periphery.

Our stories are our past. They are the fibers weaved into the fabric of the person we are today. We become better, stronger, and more resilient through our past. Our past need not define our future. We need not be victims of our past; we can instead use its lessons to stand taller and be more resilient in the present and future.

I stayed true to the two things I mentioned earlier and encourage you to do the same. Ask yourself: *What fills your heart, and what breaks it?*

When you live from your core values, you are more able to define what you stand for. You are more likely to attract the right team, the right customers, and the right people in your life. You will have a stronger understanding of your purpose and mission.

And when that is all aligned, my friends, this will make you UNSTOPPABLE.

Grieving, not All is Lost: Finding Hope and Healing Amidst Loss

Delisa Smith

DeLisa Smith, widely known as "Dee-Dee," is a multifaceted individual who has made a significant impact as a TV personality, innovator, award-winning speaker, and entrepreneur. Throughout her career, DeLisa has uplifted audiences with her remarkable talents, ranging from musical impersonations to motivational speaking.

Driven to inspire and make a difference, DeLisa spreads a message of love and acceptance, aiming to impact and positively influence those she encounters. Her high-energy communication style is relatable and universally appealing, resonating with diverse audiences.

DeLisa's educational journey includes the completion of her undergraduate studies at the University of Central Arkansas, followed by the attainment of a master's degree in business management. As a proud member of Sigma Gamma Rho Sorority Inc., she possesses a natural affinity for the stage and has honed her skills as a performer. One notable appearance includes her feature on *The Steve Harvey Show* during the exhilarating Battle of the Sexes segment. Additionally, DeLisa has graced the screens of *Ellen's Game of Games* and *The Ellen DeGeneres Show*, further solidifying her presence in the entertainment industry.

DeLisa's philosophy can be encapsulated in her own words: "I just want to be the best version of me. I don't want to say *if I had to do it all over again.*" This mindset reflects her unwavering commitment to personal growth and embracing every experience that has contributed to shaping her into the exceptional individual she is today.

In addition to her various pursuits, DeLisa serves as the president of FemaleRUS, an organization dedicated to supporting women and promoting small businesses through networking platforms. Furthermore, she excels as a financial consultant with World Financial Group, leveraging her expertise to assist individuals in managing their financial matters effectively.

With a deep-rooted passion for empowering women, DeLisa has dedicated her time and efforts to creating opportunities for women to come together, network, promote their talents, and share valuable resources through FemaleRUS. As the co-founder and president of FemaleRUS, she fosters a strong sense of community and collaboration among women, allowing them to join forces and support one another in every aspect of life.

***

I often get asked two questions:

What's the secret to your success? and, *How did you find yourself in the position you are in today?*

My response is always simple, quick, and decisive: I am here by the Grace of God!

I believe am not the hero of my own story. Anything good I've done, any accolades I've received have been because my steps have been ordered by the Highest. In the grand tapestry of life, we often find that our journeys are shaped by the challenges we face and the love and support we receive from those around us. My story is no different. While I may not consider myself the hero of my narrative, I have learned the true meaning of resilience and the transformative power of community.

Throughout my life, I have endured numerous hardships and experienced profound loss and grief. The passing of my mother, partner, grandparents, aunts, uncles, and cousins left me shattered and vulnerable. The pain I felt was indescribable, and it seemed my world had caged me in. I have seen that in each of those moments, I was not alone. The Lord always placed people in my path to help me through each life event. Amid my despair, I found solace in the unwavering love and support of my family and friends.

When we lose someone we love, the pain can be paralyzing. It weighs heavily on our hearts, leaving us feeling lost and alone. The thought of confronting this pain head-on can be terrifying, and to shield ourselves from its intensity, we may choose to keep busy or distract ourselves with various tasks. However, I have realized that avoiding grief does not make it disappear. Instead, it merely postpones it, allowing it to manifest differently and potentially leading to emotional, physical, and psychological trauma.

As I faced more losses, the pain compounded, and it became increasingly difficult to find the strength to carry on. It was during these dark times that I turned to my community and my faith in God. They became my pillars of strength, offering comfort through their words and actions. Even when I struggled to believe in myself, their belief in me allowed me to see glimmers of hope amidst the despair. They reminded me of the resilience I possessed within, even when I felt like giving up.

With this support team, I have been able to excel in my career, earn an advanced degree, develop philanthropic pursuits, and assume leadership positions in my church and other nonprofits. Instead of allowing my spirit to be crushed by grief, I am thriving. Yes, dark moments are unavoidable, but they are necessary.

In my journey, I have understood that strength does not always manifest in heroic acts. True strength lies in our ability to lean on others when we need support, in allowing ourselves to be vulnerable, and in accepting the love and care that others offer. I have experienced firsthand the power of community and the profound impact of compassion and empathy on one's healing journey.

The heroes in my story are the friends, family, and loved ones who have lifted me when I couldn't stand on my own. Their love, understanding, and encouragement have shaped me into who I am today. They have taught me that my story is not defined solely by the hardships I have faced, but also by the strength and support I have received from those who believe in my capacity to overcome.

As I continue to navigate through life's challenges, I carry with me the valuable lessons learned from my support system. Their love has taught me that it is okay to lean on others, to ask for help when needed, and to draw strength from those around me. In doing so, I have discovered my durability and the power of unity in the face of adversity.

While my story may be marked by loss and grief, it is also a testament to the transformative power of support and compassion. I have been shaped by the love and care of those who have walked beside me. Together, we have weathered storms and emerged stronger, proving that in the grand tapestry of life, no one walks alone.

In leaving my mark, I have found solace and purpose in acts of service. By extending a helping hand to others, by being there for them during their own struggles, I am making a positive difference in the world. The power of unity and compassion can create ripples of change that extend far beyond what we can imagine. Through my acts of service, I am not only leaving a mark, but also finding fulfillment and meaning in my own life.

I am the co-founder and president of FemaleRUS, an organization created by women, for women. With a deep-rooted passion for empowering women, I have dedicated my time and efforts to creating opportunities for women to come together, network, promote their talents, and share valuable resources. Through FemaleRUS, we foster a strong sense of community and collaboration among women, allowing them to join forces and support one another in every aspect of life.

I have been fortunate to volunteer with the nonprofit organization Passion Rescue Mission, which is dedicated to serving the underserved community in Haiti. Through this organization, I have had the opportunity to make a meaningful impact by providing assistance and support to those in need. Whether distributing food, organizing medical clinics, or providing uniforms to children, Passion Rescue Mission is committed to improving the lives of the underprivileged in Haiti.

Additionally, I am also involved with the nonprofit organization Project Lenity, which focuses on small children and widows in Africa. This initiative recognizes the challenges that widows face in providing for their households and aims to empower them with a sustainable source of income. By providing goats, Project Lenity supports widows and children by encouraging self-sufficiency and long-term stability within their communities.

My story is one of resilience and the transformative power of support orchestrated and blessed by the best! I may not be the hero in my own story, but I am the hero in someone else's life. I am shaped by the love and care of those who have lifted me up. Together, we have faced loss and grief, and together, we have emerged stronger. In life, we find that no one walks alone, and by leaving our mark through acts of service, we can make a lasting impact on the world.

Being the hero in someone else's life is not only an act of kindness; it is an opportunity for personal growth, understanding, and fulfillment. By seeing the world through someone else's eyes, we cultivate empathy, spread hope, and inspire others. So, let us embrace this role with open hearts and open minds, knowing that a small act of kindness can make a world of difference to someone who feels alone. In the words of Helen Keller, "Alone, we can do so little; together, we can do so much."

Sometimes, all it takes is a helping hand or a kind word to uplift someone who feels alone or helpless. By being the hero in someone else's life, we have the power to offer hope and bring about positive change. Whether it's volunteering, lending a sympathetic ear, or extending a helping hand, small acts of kindness can have a profound impact on someone's life.

From Seoul to Fort Myers with a Layover in Sweden

Marie J. Grasmeier

Founder of Grasmeier Business Consulting, Marie is a certified public accountant, certified management accountant, certified global management accountant, and registered trust and estate practitioner.

Marie specializes in assisting foreign investors with their US tax and compliance needs and enjoys working with entrepreneurs through the entire lifecycle of a business from start-up to succession planning. She also advises real estate investors on tax strategies and was invited to contribute to the collaborative book project and national bestseller, *Wealth for Women: Conversations with the Team That Creates the Dream.*

Volunteering in the local community is important for Marie who is a graduate of Leadership Lee County and is active in many charitable and civic organizations. She is currently the treasurer of the Southwest Florida Chapter of STEP International and chair of the Diversity and Inclusion Committee for the Florida Gulf Coast to Heartland Chapter of the American Red Cross.

Marie has been an active volunteer for the American Red Cross for 22 years in various capacities, including board member and board chair. She has been honored with the President of the United States Gold Volunteer Service Award for her work with the organization.

Recent recognitions include International Tax Advisor of the Year in the United States of America by the International Advisory Experts, inaugural Women in Business honoree by Gulfshore Business Magazine, and APEX finalist by the Greater Fort Myers Chamber of Commerce.

Marie is a proud naturalized citizen, minority women business owner, fitness instructor, and runner who loves her family and friends.

***

South Korean by birth, Swedish by adoption, and American by choice. My three nationalities represent three distinct phases of my life, and even though each has come with much hardship, I'm grateful for the experiences and the resilience each one has brought.

I rarely speak about my upbringing and childhood as it makes me uncomfortable. If someone inquires, I generally summarize it quickly by stating that I was adopted from Korea, grew up in Sweden, and came to the US as an au pair with the intention of becoming an international student. In one sentence that explains my Asian looks, my Scandinavian accent, and the fact that I'm not well versed in American pop culture dating back prior to 1993.

I was found in a church when I was about seven days old in Seoul, South Korea. No note, no locket, just a completely abandoned newborn left to the mercy of kind spirits and compassionate hearts. I spent time in an orphanage and was moved to foster care until I was placed for international adoption. I have read some social workers' notes stating that I was content, always looking for food, and very friendly toward anyone giving me attention. When I at one point read this to my husband he chuckled and said, "Sounds about right, pretty much like now."

At eight months of age, I flew over the North Pole as an unaccompanied minor and arrived in Sweden where I was raised by tall fair Scandinavians. Of course, I loved my dad and still love my mom, but it would be a lie to say that I had a harmonious life after the age of nine (I really don't remember much prior to that age, and I think it's part of my survival mechanism). Out of respect for my parents, I'm not going to discuss details here, but it is no secret that my dad was an alcoholic, my mom had serious health problems, and they divorced unamicably when I was 13. Perhaps because of my situation at home, my friends and hobbies became very important to me. I was always involved in activities and saw life as a competition where I had to excel. It didn't matter if it was art, music, skiing, running, or academics; I always felt I had to prove myself, gain respect, and perhaps most importantly, earn approval.

After finishing tenth grade in Sweden, I had an opportunity to travel abroad as a foreign exchange student. I jumped at the chance, mostly because two of my best friends were going, and if they left, I'd be left alone. I completed my senior high school year in Maryland, and it was life-changing. I will share a specific story that made me appreciate and love the Land of Opportunity.

It was the first day in math class, and the teacher explained the syllabus, his expectations, and the grading policy. English is my second language, and I wasn't sure that I had understood the grading policy correctly so after class, I asked him how to earn an A in class. He responded: "All you have to do is to get a 90% or above and you'll get an A." Wow, what? I simply could not believe it. If it was that easy, wouldn't everyone earn an A, and how was that possible?

I was used to the Swedish grading system where in a group of approximately 30 students the teacher must award grades according to a flat top bell curve. After ninth grade, Swedish students must choose a direction and concentration such as sciences, technology, economics, social studies, sports, or language. I was in the science program, so generally high-performing middle schoolers would choose this or the technology program. Earning an A in any class involved active class participation, long open-ended essay questions subjectively graded by the teacher—and frankly, a lot of sucking up. It also meant staying after class and showing knowledge in areas outside the class material.

I'm not the smartest cookie around, but I do know how to follow directions, and that in combination with drive and work ethic got me good grades. When I mentor students today, this is one of the important messages that I try to convey: it's not about your IQ. It's about your commitment to achieving your goals.

Once I graduated high school in the US, I had two more years of school to finish in Sweden. I couldn't wait to finish so I could come back and start college. I had tried an internship at the local hospital and quickly realized that the medical profession was not for me. I wanted to wear suits and heels and look fabulous going to work like Amanda on *Melrose Place*. Having no idea how to accomplish this, I packed my big red hardcase Samsonite and left for the US without a visa to take care of two young children with the goal of eventually enrolling in college.

At that time, I earned $100 per week, and all my worldly possessions fit in that suitcase, but I had no worries; I woke up every day wondering how anyone living in beautiful Florida could ever be in a bad mood. During this time, I met my now husband of 27 years, and I enrolled in the College of Business at Florida Atlantic University with an undeclared major. My guidance counselor noted that I did well in my accounting classes and suggested I get a degree in that since "accounting is the universal language of business." I took her advice, finished my master's, and got the CPA designation before starting my first job at a regional accounting firm headquartered in Orlando.

During my first professional years, I learned a lot, and was fortunate to have great mentors. But I also realized that going to work in a skirt suit and pantyhose wasn't as glamorous as it was on TV. I was eager to learn and had a goal of becoming a partner at the firm as soon as possible. However, life happens, and I left that firm to join another based in Fort Myers. Seven years later, both firms were acquired by a national company. At that time, I had a sizeable portfolio of clients that I served and loved my job, but I was starting to feel the clock ticking. There was a "mommy track" at the national firm, but I didn't see anyone making partners, and I wasn't happy with the layers of management.

For almost two years, my husband took care of our daughter while I was commuting and putting in long hours. An opportunity came along, and before we knew, it he was deploying to the Middle East. I finally had a nice excuse to quit my job. I was now in charge of potty training and got a chance to bond with our girl. For a split second I thought of retiring, but the orphan in me whispered in my ear, "You have to do more, you have to prove yourself, start your own practice, run the business the way you want, serve your clients like you want to be served, and still be the best mom you can be."

Here I am, 14 years later, and I'm humbled by the recognition received by my peers, and awards received in the community. I don't really know how it happened, but I do know that I get up every day trying to do the best I can. I wish I still had the red suitcase, as it represents the true American Dream for me. However, during a time when I was in school, and we were struggling financially, it went to the pawn shop along with a few family jewelry pieces that I would do almost anything to get back now. I've learned not to look back, only look forward. I could have buried myself in pity so many times, wondering why my parents abandoned me, hating myself for not being tall, blond, and skinny, wondering why I had to deal with infertility, and so on. But that would not accomplish anything but waste time and energy.

Hardships are difficult, heartbreaking, and awful to live through. But it's how your ship is sailing out of each that defines you and makes you stronger for the next one.

I'm proud to call myself Korean, Swedish, and American. My daughter and I just came back from our fifth trip to Sweden and we're now planning our first to South Korea next year. I'm thankful for the opportunity to teach her about her culture and heritage and tell her about all the doors that are available and ready to swing wide open for her in the future. In my heart, I know that I provided her with the best start in life that I was able to give her; that's all I wanted, and it's what's most important to me. <3

THE PATH TO BELIEVING IN YOURSELF

Samreen Mongillo

Dr. Samreen Mongillo is a physical therapist and a success and life coach. She earned her doctorate in physical therapy from Florida Gulf Coast University (FGCU) and a master's in adult education from Virginia Commonwealth University. Additionally, she holds an Advanced Belief Clearing Practitioner Certification from The Clearing Academy (Dr. Joe Vitale) and a Personal Training Certification from ACE (The American Council on Exercise) and is a certified Jack Canfield Success Principles Trainer. Dr. Mongillo teaches people how to own their power, cultivate a strong mindset, and effectively manage stress. She provides practical tools for fostering more joy, a healthier lifestyle, and greater life balance. She believes that our mindset and our beliefs are essential factors in manifesting greater happiness, health, and joy. Dr. Samreen Mongillo's true passion is about coaching individuals to believe in their self-worth, to be the most confident version of themselves, to connect to their highest potential, and help them live their best lives.

Dr. Mongillo lives with her husband and her son in beautiful Naples, Florida. She is passionate about helping people improve the quality of their lives and dreams of a world where people pursue a happy and healthy lifestyle with love and purpose. Dr. Mongillo will teach you how to transform the quality of your life.

http://www.coachingbysamreen.com

https://linkedin.com/in/dr-samreen-sofia-mongillo-7ba3b97a

https://www.facebook.com/coachingbysamreen

https://www.instagram.com/selfcarecoach_mindset

***

History is full of countless stories of individuals who not only overcame adversity but also used those challenges as catalysts for success. Adversity can either make or break us. Regardless of our circumstances, I firmly believe that we can rise above any challenge. What matters most is how we respond to the obstacles that come our way.

Every one of us has the capacity to cultivate mental toughness and build resilience to weather life's storms and challenges. Trust me... if I can do it, anybody can!

Reflecting on my own experiences, I realize that every challenge I've encountered has not only made me more resilient but has also paved the way for greater wisdom and inner strength. As Alain de Botton wisely stated, "A good half of the art of living is resilience."

Over the years I have learned to overcome adversity and emerged stronger as a result. Because of these experiences, I am passionate about helping people to believe in themselves and embrace their power. When you see your inner light and beauty, your life transforms. Too many people put their self-care last and accept stress as the norm, not realizing its debilitating long-term impact. Prolonged stress not only steals our happiness, but also damages our health, relationships, and overall quality of life. It is also a leading cause of many chronic illnesses such as heart disease, diabetes, cancer, and mental health problems.

Life's challenges transform us, forcing us to dig deeper and find a strength that we never knew existed within us. The challenges I faced along my own journey—especially having debilitating chronic headaches for years, which I eventually overcame—motivated me to explore the underlying causes of stress and its impact on chronic illness.

I truly believe that a lack of self-love is at the root of chronic stress.

New Age thought leaders like Bruce Lipton, Louise Hay, and other pioneers in this field have arrived at similar conclusions. They suggest that the body listens and responds to our deepest thoughts and beliefs, which reside within our subconscious. It seems they are correct in proposing that the energetic frequency of our bodies always aligns with our thoughts and beliefs. The mind and body are intricately interconnected. Recurring negative thoughts can lead to a state of chronic stress and then eventually result in physical symptoms. A low opinion of oneself results in negative beliefs and negative self-talk. This can result in chronic stress, ultimately diminishing our joy, health, and overall well-being in life.

During my teenage years, I developed a strong passion for fitness and motivating others to prioritize their health. I was inspired by watching trainers like Denise Austin on her Lifetime shows, where she provided tips on cultivating a positive mindset, exercising, and embracing a healthy lifestyle. Alongside pursuing my bachelor's degree in communications and master's in adult education, I worked as a personal trainer. I loved helping clients achieve their health goals through weightlifting and cardiovascular exercises. It was so rewarding for me that it led me to pursue a doctorate in physical therapy a few years later. I had found my calling. I enjoyed every aspect of this career, from rehabilitating individuals to motivating them to live a healthy lifestyle and achieve their fullest potential.

After practicing as a physical therapist for over a decade, my focus shifted to understanding the underlying causes of chronic stress. Throughout my years of treating physical therapy patients, I observed an intriguing trend. Those who experienced chronic stress and led unhealthy lifestyles had poorer recovery outcomes compared to patients of the same age and diagnosis. This recurring pattern motivated me to investigate the root cause of chronic stress, which I discovered to be a major obstacle to the recovery of many patients. I wanted to help people on a broader scale. Consequently, I established my life coaching business to help individuals manage their stress levels and improve their mental and physical well-being.

Each setback I have encountered in my life has given me greater inner strength. From my parents' divorce when I was six years old, to experiencing burnout and enduring years of chronic headaches, and recently, facing the harsh reality of my mother's stage 4 cancer diagnosis, these experiences compelled me to delve deeper and discover an inner strength that I never knew existed. Each setback in my life served as a driving force for profound transformation, pushing me to prioritize my self-care. Through these challenges, I learned that prioritizing my mental, physical, and spiritual health allowed me to confront life's obstacles with greater empowerment. Making self-care a priority became my most effective defense mechanism against stress.

For years, I suffered from debilitating chronic headaches that caused extreme pain. I wanted relief. But despite seeking help from various holistic practitioners, I found no solutions. Then, I had a realization: It wasn't my circumstances or the overwhelming chronic headaches that needed to change for my life to improve—it was *me* who needed to change. Once I started to practice turning my focus inward, I began to see improvements in my chronic headaches. I needed to examine how I perceived myself, and it turned out that my intuition had been correct all along. I had to start listening to my body and prioritizing my self-care needs.

I wondered how things had gotten so bad. I realized that my relentless pursuit of success over the years had caused me to neglect my self-care needs. I was constantly doing and achieving, rather than simply being. This tendency to overachieve and work harder than anyone around me had come at the expense of my self-care. Perhaps my failure to recognize my self-worth and prioritize my needs had negatively impacted my health. Could this behavior have played a major role in my years of chronic headaches?

Turns out that trying to prove myself by overachieving and not prioritizing my true needs left me feeling anything but healthy, vibrant, or energized.

I realized that I had a choice: I could either start taking ownership of my own health by prioritizing my self-care or continue to suffer from debilitating, painful headaches. This really motivated me to take control of my health by watching what I ate, getting adequate sleep, exercising regularly, meditating consistently, and simplifying my overwhelming to-do list. I began making these positive changes in my mindset and daily habits.

My experiences essentially drove me to discover my purpose in life: to help people manage chronic stress and achieve their greatest health mentally, physically, and spiritually. I do this by sharing the tools that helped me overcome chronic stress and discover joy. After all, our health is our greatest asset and affects every aspect of our lives.

One of the most valuable life lessons I have learned is that, regardless of our circumstances, we always have the power to choose our response. We always have a choice. We can choose a healthy thought. At any given moment, we can choose to focus on love over fear. We can choose to believe in ourselves and recognize our true capabilities, or we can put ourselves down. We always have this choice. Ultimately, the key to managing stress and improving our well-being lies in strengthening our mindset and developing daily habits that promote optimal health and joy. If we do this, we can overcome any stressor that life throws our way.

I love this quote from Lucille Ball, "Love yourself and everything else falls into place." When we love ourselves fiercely, our thoughts and actions will align with that love, profoundly influencing our well-being. Recognizing our worth, prioritizing our self-care, and meeting our own needs, have a tremendously positive impact on our mental and physical health.

I believe that life may present us with numerous challenges, but how we handle them is what truly matters. And it is essentially our thoughts that play a crucial role in shaping our responses.

When I learned to focus inward and started to cultivate greater compassion for myself, my chronic headaches dissipated.

My decision to make healthy choices improved my whole life tremendously. Yes, I still face significant life stressors today, but self-love and cultivating healthy habits served as a strong buffer against stress.

When it comes to shaping outcomes in our lives, our mindset is incredibly powerful.

As Viktor Frankl once said, "Between stimulus and response, there is a pause, and in that pause lies our opportunity to choose our response." Frankl, a Holocaust survivor and author of *Man's Search for Meaning*, found moments of joy even in the darkest circumstances. Despite the horrors he faced, he focused on his love for his wife and experienced joy. If he could find joy in such dire circumstances, then anyone can.

My journey led me to become a physical therapist and establish my life coaching business. I am currently writing a book meant to help people discover joy and health by cultivating greater self-love, a positive mindset, and healthy habits. In it, I provide practical tools and solutions to help people find joy and break free from chronic stress. The message that I teach my clients is that as you learn to love yourself, you are essentially becoming your own best friend. It is through this self-love that you unlock the key to success. Self-love will lead to positive beliefs, positive self-talk, positive actions, and results in life. It is our choice to rise above, dig deeper, and emerge stronger on the other side.

Overcoming my own setbacks inspired me to empower others to tap into their inner strength, experience deeper joy, and create a life they love. My message is this: even if joy seems distant, you can still find it. Ultimately, the decision is yours. You can choose positive thoughts over negative ones, love and gratitude over fear and worry. It all comes down to treating yourself as your own best friend because you matter. You are deserving and worthy of a fulfilling life! Believe in every fiber of your being that you are a unique part of the universe and deserve happiness and love.

With only one life to live, prioritize your relationship with yourself. If you can learn to love yourself wholeheartedly, and become your best friend, it will help you truly discover joy!

An excerpt from *21 Years and 29 Days: A Sentencing I Allowed to Happen*

Marjorie "MJ" Kasell-Johnson

Born in Raleigh, NC, in 1975, Marjorie (MJ) grew up in nearby Cary with her parents and two siblings. As a young girl, MJ was surrounded by her mother's contagious love of books. MJ wanted to be a writer from an early age but never shared her work for fear of embarrassing scrutiny from her family. Her love of the classics, travel, and history came in handy as she took on marketing positions early on in her career.

After finding success in the modeling industry, MJ was hired as an agency director in Charlotte, NC where she met and married her ex-husband of 21 years. From that marriage, she has two daughters.

In 2001, MJ moved to Naples, Fla., with her ex-husband and daughters. Over the next several years, she worked in a series of roles for different companies including not-for-profit organizations and Fortune 500 companies. She worked as a director of development, executive area director, and sales and marketing director, and then eventually landed in the real estate industry.

MJ is a published author, 40 Under 40 award winner, chair of 17 not-for-profit galas, and past board member for multiple organizations. She has been lauded with the Apex Women in Business, Person to Watch, Trailblazer, and National Top Agent for a Fortune 500 company honors.

MJ has built a record of success in developing marketing campaigns, strategies, and solutions.

One would think while watching the replay of the last several years since she said, "no more" to her ex-husband, every obstacle was thrown in her way trying to block healing and success. She had to learn how to make her own personal decisions, raise her children on zero child support, face the world with a destroyed personal and professional reputation, and then lose her home in a hurricane; every hindrance almost knocked her down. In her own words: "Yes, I went through hell, but I always stood up stronger, played my cards right, and never downplayed my talents or degraded my integrity."

Today, MJ lives a fulfilling professional and personal life in Naples, Fla., with a modern blended family of beloved daughters, Eric (the love of her life), and their fur babies. She stays close to friends and family. She continues to heal but still laughs daily, loves without fearful restraint, and recognizes her blessings. She loves offshore fishing, spending time on the family's weekend ranch, traveling, and finally *feeling like she is actually worth something, after 21 years and 29 days of being told she wasn't.*

***

December 1995

It was the holiday season of 1995. I was living alone, and newer to the Charlotte area. I had just landed my first "big girl" job as an agency director for a modeling agency and the world seemed ready for me to take over. I had been involved in the modeling industry for most of my younger years, so being around attractive charismatic people was normal and comfortable.

I had heard of the new, immensely handsome talent that had blue eyes and black hair, but I had not placed any emphasis on meeting him because there were dozens of "him" already in our talent pool. After weeks of hearing about him and having never met, plus a very hectic schedule, the buzz died down and he was nothing but yesterday's news for me. However, it was as if something told me to look up; and when I did, we locked eyes for what seemed like an eternity... and oh my, yes, he was different. At that moment, my life changed forever.

From our first date on, we were inseparable. The *I love yous* flowed constantly, followed by a quick engagement. Within 14 months we were married. It was all such a whimsical blur that the constant red flags I saw were ignored: no friends whatsoever, a severe outcast and introvert, not close with his own family, and always pressuring me to isolate myself from everyone. His communication was manipulative, and he consistently one-upped me in front of others. The lying, and financial control, became normal and if questioned, would result in his actions being my fault. If I disagreed with him, he would block my movement and repeat his opinion repeatedly, then he would preach for hours until

I would finally agree with him so I could get away. He also had an ability that he often bragged about of being able to walk away from relationships and never look back or care about the well-being of others.

Within the first month of our relationship, a major red flag incident occurred. His ex-girlfriend whom he dated for two years was well-liked by his family and held in high regard by them. She appeared troubled about their break-up which resulted in multiple calls to his home, messages being relayed to him by his family from her, and letters mailed to the residence. At the time, I considered it stalking, but looking back on it, she wasn't stalking him; she just wanted answers and closure.

At that time, I never lacked self-confidence, so I had no problem with this. I encouraged him to speak with her. He refused. Finally, while I sat beside him, he answered her call. I can still hear her words, as she tried to comprehend his emotionless words. She asked him why he wouldn't call her back, why he broke up with her after they spent every day together for two years, how he could just go cold and dark as if she had died. His reply was cold and cutting, "I don't love you. I never did and I never will." I could hear her sobs and her saying, "You said you loved me, we were going to get married, then you just vanished." He hung up, looked at me, and said, "That's done, let's go get some dinner." He then stood up and walked out. There was zero compassion nor care, but I was in love and all the red flags didn't matter.

A few years later, our first daughter was born. This is a time when most people are excited to grow together. I was terrified. Like all new parents, we went through the struggles of parenting a newborn, but things were still off. He didn't play with our daughter unless encouraged by me. He often told me he didn't marry me to have children, he married me to be with me, not our daughter, and I was to put him first. The narcissistic tactics of isolation, character assassination, withholding attention, manipulation, and eventual lying about infidelity broke me down to immense guilt and depression. It finally came to a head when he abruptly left me and our 11-month-old baby girl for three days—he just vanished, disappeared, without a word to anyone.

I filed a missing person's report. Was he dead? He eventually came home from her house, the first mistress of many. He told me I drove him to her, and that "he just needed some space." It was my fault that he needed space, a different scene to clear his head. I can't explain what his thoughts were, but it appeared that his logic was that it's completely normal for a husband and father of a baby to go missing for three days with zero communication with anyone. This instance and many more would be blamed on me.

His solution was for us to become closer: we were to move three states away from all the negative influences of our family and my friends to save our marriage.

When I crossed the state line, my gut and part of my soul died. I knew I would never get away from him. I was moving away from my entire support system and life as I knew it. I was terrified and stuck, but I was determined to hold my family together.

After our second daughter was born, what previously had been an extreme fascination with wealth, cars, houses, and flashy things, turned into an obsession. As the years passed, if he wasn't talking about how horrible our life was because we didn't have wealth, he was talking about how we were going to get wealth, or how we could look like we had wealth. If he saw a car, boat, or house that he liked he would obsess over how to get it for hours, days, weeks. No matter how well we did in our careers financially, it was never enough. This issue was exacerbated when he started selling homes in one of the wealthiest communities in the US. He was surrounded by wealth, flashy lifestyles, and a party atmosphere with open marriages, and he was determined to have it all. And no matter how hard I protested, I was going to be his ticket to that lifestyle.

April 2015

At this time my career was continuing to skyrocket. I sat on numerous boards, chaired multiple events, and earned several local and national awards. I was even starting to have discussions about building a political career. Yes, my life at home was a mess, but in the publics eye, it was perfect. My ex-husband and I had our normal marital problems, but his obsession with kicking off a company, partying, and pushing for sex outside of our marriage, plus my father's rapidly declining health, was mentally destroying me.

Oddly, I could run businesses and boards, but I could not run the finances at home. He always had control and would spend as he saw fit. The only task I was allowed to do was to hit the online bill pay button. At first, I didn't agree with his financial management, but after years of his preaching to me, I learned to pick my battles and the finances were not one of them. As a salaried employee, my income was exact, however, he was commissioned, so the amounts fluctuated. I never knew what he was making or when he would get paid. I assumed because his spending, partying, and push for travel with other wealthy couples was in overload, he was doing well at work, but I later found out he wasn't.

One day, I opened the family computer, and the screen was frozen on an account I did not know about. There were thousands of dollars in it! I immediately called him for an explanation. His reply was that he was going to surprise me with it and invest in the market and in his personal company for our retirement. This snowballed into me uncovering unpaid bills and learning that he was using money from the company I worked for to pay bills... plus there was much more. He promised the money would get paid back to my company when he got paid, and for us to use the funds temporarily until he could pay everything back, but the board uncovered everything before that could happen. There I was with a husband, children, and a public reputation about to be destroyed, plus my father was days away from dying. I had no way to help any of it.

As the detective's report came out wth my ex-husband's name and eye-witness reports were logged showing him delivering stolen checks and sending payments to his accounts, my attorney called me to come in and discuss my ex-husband's involvement in the crime. Prior to the meeting, my ex pleaded with me to take the fall because apparently his reputation was "already ruined" and he "needed to stay in the clear to support our family." At first, I vehemently rejected the idea of taking full responsibility for this theft. However, like a police interrogation that lasted for hours, out of exhaustion, frustration, and many years of accepted manipulation from him, I agreed. The next day as tears streamed down my face, I told my attorney that my ex-husband was completely innocent. He didn't believe me and said the facts were there in the detective's report. I kept to my story and left his office.

June 6, 2017

The courtroom was quiet. The media, board members, and upcoming case members had their eyes on me. My ex-husband was absent because he (his words) "needed to stay away from the case and not be recognized because it could ruin his reputation." I wanted him or someone I knew there with me. I was scared speechless and literally had no one to look at for reassurance. While my mind was racing and tears streamed down my face, I heard the judge say, "Mrs. Johnson, do you have anything to say." In what felt like a lifetime, every thought came to my head. I wanted to scream out, "Yes! I have something to say. I'm innocent. This is all a mistake. Over the last 21 years, I've been trying to be a good wife, mother, leader, and an example to others. I want to make everyone happy and proud of me. I'm in this mess because of him. He's sitting inside of our beautiful home right now. The home I've worked my ass off for eating the food I cooked for him, wearing the clean clothes I washed and put away, probably calling one of the couples he wanted to go away with and planning a trip with them while I'm in jail and the kids at their grandparents." I wanted to scream, "This isn't real; this isn't happening." Instead, I wiped my tears away and said, "No, I have nothing to say." The judge said, "Ok, Mrs. Johnson, you are to turn yourself in immediately for 29 days of county jail. Please follow the bailiff."

June 12, 2017

I have been in jail for one week. Today is my first day with a pen, paper, soap, toothpaste, a toothbrush, and pads for my period that started a few days ago. My husband has visited me once and said he was working hard, cleaning and reorganizing our house, his business, and our accounts while I've been gone. He said I shouldn't worry; his business partner has been helping and she's been doing a great job diligently coming to the house every day, sometimes staying over if needed. He also said he was super busy and couldn't come often. My gut said something major was going on, but my heart said he had our best interest at heart... he did... didn't he...

For 21 years and 29 days, I allowed a sentencing of narcissistic and sociopathic abuse. My own "sentencing" eventually led to a real-life incarceration, quickly followed by a textbook sociopathic ending: he formulated a cold, calculated plan to walk away and never look back once.

My children and I no longer provided any worth to him.

Abuse and narcissism are big buzzwords, so broad and regularly used that the intensity of their meaning has been diminished. If someone does something you find inconsiderate or selfish, those actions do not make them an abusive or narcissistic person. Yes, people can show abusive, narcissistic tendencies at times. But recognizing and having a clear understanding of textbook, diagnosable, abusive, sociopathic narcissism and how to survive and heal from its wrath is why I'm sharing this excerpt from my book *21 Years and 29 Days*. To learn about my story, please read *21 Years and 29 Days*.

Never Clocked Out

Katie Edmonds Peters

Born and raised in Fort Myers, Katie Edmonds Peters has made her way to the title of top ultra-luxury real estate agents in her hometown. As the cofounder of HAVEN GROUP, Katie leads a team of 10 agents and services all over Southwest Florida.

But real estate was not always Katie's top priority—as a mother of three, she spent years building a family with her husband, Trey, and their three beautiful children: Dru (10), Ambrose (9), and Virginia (6). When it came time to venture outside stay-at-home-mom life, Katie earned her real estate license in just 12 days. With a degree and background in fashion and marketing, and six years running a household, Katie then channeled all of her expertise into selling luxury homes, boasting $53 million in sales in 2022.

With a shrewd understanding of her area, and the moxie of a mother, Katie is unmatched in her ability to connect a client with their dream home. Her attention to detail, ability to read people, and familiarity with Southwest Florida set her apart from her peers.

Prior to starting a family, Katie was able to travel, work in a wide range of retail positions, and witness her father act as CEO of a major clothing store. She credits her success in real estate to her life experiences, and firmly believes that timing is everything—she is where she's meant to be, and she's crushing it. What she lacks in years, she makes up for with savvy, consideration, and empathy.

***

My father was one of six and my mother one of five children—all of them raised by powerhouse moms. "Matriarch" was a term I grew up understanding well, and I had very real and present women to define it. I knew from the beginning that I wanted to follow in my grandmothers' footsteps, to raise a family, and to mold and support them the way the women before me had. My older sister and I could not be more different, but she is my rock. The two of us would go to the ends of the earth for each other. It is because of her that I reconnected with a childhood sweetheart at his sister's (a friend of my sister, Healy) wedding in 2010. He has been my husband for seven years and we have three children: Dru (10), Ambrose (9) and Virginia (6).

Having grown up with my mother, the youngest of her four siblings, as a stay-at-home mom, it seemed a natural path to take with my three littles. When I tell you I leaned in, I mean I leaned IN. My kids wanted for nothing, had 110% of my attention, participated in countless sports, traveled, and were well-read and well-fed. I poured everything I had into raising the type of family and being the kind of mother I knew my foremothers to be. I have always loved babies and children and was (and still am) the first to host a sleepover or chaperone a school trip.

When my sister adopted her infant son around the same time as I had my second, I breastfed my son, Ambrose, and pumped milk for my newborn nephew until he was six months old. My entire life was raising babies, and I loved every second of it.

On the flip side of that coin—I was also very aware of and very inspired by my father's success. Behind every stay-at-home mom, is a spouse who provides financially. My father came from very little and is entirely self-made. He started from the bottom, driving a truck and working in the warehouse of a building supply company in 1981, and retired as president, CEO, and chairman of the board of a major women's clothing company in 2009. He hasn't stopped working a single day into that retirement. I was blessed to inherit each of my parents' finest (and, at times, the arguably "undesirable") attributes, and as soon as my youngest started school, I knew it was time to refocus my energy toward a professional setting.

There had always been a sleeping beast inside of me, ready to awaken.

My husband, Trey, and I purchased a home in 2019 and, true to form, used a childhood friend of Healy's, Joey, as our realtor. I had known Joey since I was in middle school, and, as a result of that family friendship, was privy to every aspect of the home-buying process. I was fascinated and inspired: I went on to earn my real estate license in just 12 days—before we had even closed on our house. My now business partner, Joey, likes to retell the joke that I "wasn't getting any part of his commission" for our new home in Fort Myers!

I got a job at the brokerage Joey had been with for several years and spent a year and a half learning everything I could from him. I very quickly knew that real estate fit me like a glove and would be my lifelong career. Timing is everything, and it felt like every skill or trait that I had acquired up to that point was useful and helped me thrive in business. In 2021, Joey and I both left that brokerage, and founded HAVEN GROUP. We managed a whopping $53 million in sales in 2022. Joey and I now run a team of ten agents, servicing all of Southwest Florida. I know in my heart that my professional success can be traced back to the work ethic my father instilled in me and the way generations on either side were brought up with compassion, empathy, and tenacity.

Before I reconnected with Trey, I lived in New York City for eight years and attended The Fashion Institute of Technology. I held a handful of positions in the fashion industry, mainly in casting, before irrevocably deciding that it wasn't the industry for me. I moved out of the city when I became pregnant with Dru in 2012, and he was born in Newport News, Virginia. The three of us lived in my parents' hometown there for one year, before returning to our roots in Fort Myers. Dru is an old soul and a typical eldest sibling—responsible, driven, and the ultimate sports enthusiast. Ambrose was born in 2014 in Fort Myers, but he is my laid-back Virginia boy. He loves fishing, hunting, and cooking. Virginia, "Ginnie," is our wild card! She is outgoing, sassy, and loving, and at six years old is the undisputed queen of the household. (And very likely the entire neighborhood!)

Part of what molded me as a child was spending time in Virginia with my cousins. I'm sure they'd all agree we were more like siblings than cousins—a relationship developed because of the closeness of our parents and their siblings, and their commitment to making sure we spent as much time together as possible. There are eight of us on my mother's side and five on my father's. My maternal grandmother, our "Nanny," turned 96 this summer and spent her birthday with 15 of her 16 great-grandchildren. When we aren't visiting extended family, my own children are blessed to live just two houses down from Trey's parents—their "Bumpy Ma" and "Papi." Both Trey's sister and my own live less than half an hour away, as do my own parents—"Nana" and "Papa" to the kids. It fills my heart to be able to provide the same sort of family closeness (both in proximity and relationship) for my kids that made me the woman I am today.

These family bonds are what I lean on now that I'm a full-time working mom. My children are growing up valuing my dedication to my career without having to sacrifice the precious adolescent years spent with kin. Being a mother, at least a good one, means never being off the clock. Real estate is not unlike that. In order to excel in either career, you must be on call 24-hours a day, seven days a week, 365 days a year. Excelling at both simultaneously comes down to time management and prioritization.

In my life, there's a fine line between "masochistic" and "self-motivated"—but I wouldn't have it any other way. I have never been busier, but it is truly what fulfills me. There are days when I show four houses, list another, close on a multi-million-dollar property, and then come home to clean up dog barf, fold laundry, make dinner, and check homework. I always say that my life is like rubbing your belly and patting your head at the same time—and you better be damn good at both.

I am acutely aware that there are women who crush it in both business and motherhood without the support system and family background that I'm blessed to have and lean on daily. I remind myself of this when I'm feeling overwhelmed. Not all of us come from nothing, or have to work our way to the top, overcoming prejudice or trauma. Even we women with the privilege of a strong family and economic foundation still must fight our asses off to be something in this world, and I will always do my absolute best to live up to the boss women and mothers before me.

One of my favorite quotes is from actor Denzel Washington, who said, "Don't just aspire to make a living, aspire to make a difference." As much as I loved being a stay-at-home mom, I always felt that I had more to contribute to this world than what I accomplished within my own home. My mother was and is an inspiration to me, and the backbone of our family. My grandmothers overcame poverty and single-parenthood to raise eleven children between them and create a loving and supportive family dynamic that has strongly influenced two generations since. I intend to make it three, and to raise this next generation with the same devotion to both home and profession that shaped me.

Who says we can't do it all?

I have tremendous career goals and I do not intend to slow down anytime soon. This train is full steam ahead.

Being born and raised in Fort Myers, I'm passionate about our city. City Council recently elected me to be on the Charter Review Committee Board. I have also volunteered throughout the years at the Community Cooperative—something my parents encouraged and insisted upon, and that I now bring my kids and their cousins to participate in. Like motherhood, being a working mom is an experience that is hard to explain to someone who hasn't lived it themselves. No matter how supportive or present your partner is, you are and will always be "mom." It doesn't matter if you worked a 12-hour day—when you walk in the door at night, everyone still turns to you and says, "What's for dinner?"

A STORY OF RESILIENCE AND DETERMINATION

Marilyn Santiago

Despite having lived in Southwest Florida for only seven years, Marilyn Santiago has quickly become one of the area's most influential figures. She has had a significant and transformative impact on both the business sector and the community. Santiago is the owner of two companies: Creative Architectural Resin Products and Sunshine Integrated Solutions. She has been recognized for her outstanding achievements and leadership with various accolades and awards, including the prestigious Apex Award, which is the most sought-after recognition for women in the region. However, what truly sets Santiago apart is her humility and sincere dedication to serving others.

***

There is a popular Spanish saying, *Más sabe el diablo por viejo que por diablo*, which translates to "The devil knows more because he is old than because he is the devil."

Whenever I hear it, it reminds me of the invaluable wisdom that comes with age. As I was invited to reflect on my own journey as the oldest (or at least one of the oldest) ladies featured in Slaying SWFL, I recognize that my longevity in this realm has equipped me with an incredible wealth of knowledge. To all you younger slayers, I hope you all embrace the power of experience.

Age provides us with countless opportunities to learn from our successes and failures. As we navigate life, we accumulate a treasure trove of lessons that can only be gained through time.

Growing up as a spoiled and entitled child, I never realized the value of hard work or the sacrifices others made for my happiness. I was really a spoiled brat, surrounded by people who catered to my every whim. I lacked appreciation; I didn't understand the value of hard work or the importance of perseverance. But as life threw lemons at me, I embarked on a process of transformation, turning those lemons into something beautiful. Gladly, life had other plans for me.

My story began when I realized that I lived in a protected and privileged bubble. When the real world hit me, it hit hard. Depression, low self-esteem, and a lack of self-respect became constants in my life. I was enrolled in a prestigious school filled with children from influential families, where I was met with name-calling and ridicule. I never understood why they called me names, as I had always been told I was beautiful... even a princess! How could they be so mean?

That prestigious school heightened the cruelty I faced from my peers. I was subjected to bullying, classism, and misogyny. Sadly, later in life, I would also experience the horrors of domestic violence.

College changed my life. I played volleyball for the university and later on, I played semiprofessionally, which not only helped my self-esteem, but also enhanced my social skills. I embraced my leadership when I became involved in the American Marketing Association. I excelled as their president, receiving multiple accolades. After graduating and landing a job in marketing, then managing four radio stations in beautiful Puerto Rico, I embarked on a career in radio and the entertainment industry that lasted over two decades.

Sadly, I soon found myself trapped in an abusive relationship. It's crazy that while I was enduring the darkest moments of my personal life, my professional life soared. My radio stations were successful in both ratings and revenue. I found myself balancing success and pain, so I learned to laugh. Through it all, I maintained my sense of humor, my laughter masking my pain... Thankfully, I broke free, discovering inner strength and resilience I never knew existed. I became determined to outsmart the challenges I faced.

After a decade of suffering, I finally found the strength to escape my toxic relationship and rebuild my life. The horrors I endured taught me the value of perseverance and hard work. I excelled in my career but encountered the harsh reality that Latinas are often underpaid compared to other demographics. I was excelling as a professional—but my salary showed otherwise. The salary gap is something we all need to join forces to fight. But for minorities, the challenge is way bigger.

So, I did what I had to do.

Determined to change my circumstances, on April 15, 2006, I decided to venture out on my own and open my own business, Sunshine Integrated Solutions, which provides strategic advice and creative services to those in need of a different perspective. (It is still in existence, though some of the offerings have changed over the years.)

Sunshine has been a great ride. Sunshine has never disappointed me.

Thanks to my company, I moved on to enjoy an exciting and fulfilling career, crossing paths with celebrities, and influencing major deals. I have been instrumental in the creation of successful startups and have helped many professionals structure their dreams and bring them to fruition. While life may not always be fair, I have learned to believe in myself and surround myself with individuals who respect and admire me.

In addition to my marketing/entertainment company, in 2015, I decided to reinvent myself, so I joined forces with my partner in life, Steven Russell, and we established Creative Architectural Resin Products, inc. We cater to construction companies and developers by designing, manufacturing, and installing nonstructural architectural elements made out of polyurethane resin.

Today, I stand as a survivor, helping others in each way I can, spreading my knowledge, and empowering the next generation. I have found a loving companion who treats me with respect and admiration. Life may not always be fair, but I will continue to change the things I cannot accept.

My life has been a journey and I am grateful for the things I have discovered about myself... here are a few highlights:

1. I am a product of the challenges I have overcome in my life. These experiences have shaped my character and made me who I am today. We all face multiple obstacles in our journey, and it is how we handle them

that defines us. Eventually, we all realize that as long as we learn the lesson, there'll be no right or wrong. Thanks to all those lessons, I have become a very kind-hearted person — unless you face me in the midst of a menopause attack... and believe me, you don't want that, ha!

2. I embody the qualities of an extrovert to the fullest. I am outspoken, humorous, confident, passionate, and quite intelligent. While some people might see me as an extraordinary woman, other individuals may perceive me as weak or lacking intelligence (when in fact, I have a 138 IQ, which is not bad at all).

3. I have zero tolerance for injustice. Unfortunately, in recent years, many people have felt empowered to showcase their uglier sides, and dealing with these injustices has not been easy. I can't stand them and sadly, since I moved to Southwest Florida, I've been subject to multiple injustices myself.

5. My ultimate goal in life is to leave a positive impact on everyone I encounter. I really hope I can make everyone feel better — so much so that sometimes I joke around telling people that I am like a walking Hallmark card! But honestly, I am blessed with the ability to see the potential in everything, and especially in people. While I may see the worst in myself (I could probably write a whole book on the topic of imposter syndrome), I always strive to see the best in others.

As I reflect on my journey, I am reminded of the quote by Angela Davis: "I'm no longer accepting the things I cannot change... I'm changing the things I cannot accept." This is now my mantra, my guiding light, my beacon of hope.

As I look back, I also cherish every moment spent with my mother. We never know when it will be the last. So, I encourage you all to appreciate and enjoy your time with your loved ones, for it is truly priceless.

No longer bound by my past, I have transformed into a force to be reckoned with. My story is proof that we can overcome the obstacles life throws at us and create our own destinies. This is my story, and it is filled with perseverance, resilience, and unyielding determination.

Breaking the Chains of Shame: A Journey of Healing and Empowerment

Sally Brumfield

I am Sally Brumfield, a dedicated and passionate development director at the best foundation of a wonderful and expansive retirement community. After a 26-year tenure in the banking industry, I embarked on a new journey, driven by my desire to make a meaningful impact on the lives of the community. My transition to this fulfilling role showcases the resilience and determination to follow my true calling of servant leadership. My journey stands as a testament that—through dedication, perseverance, reliance upon God, and a newfound sense of self-love—even the most unexpected achievements become within reach. Beyond my professional realm, I deeply value the love and support I enjoy from my husband, children, mother, extended family, and chosen loved ones.

I've learned to foster robust and nurturing relationships, characterized by warmth, care, and a lack of judgment. My message revolves around self-acceptance and unwavering love, extended to every individual in my life. Embracing the belief that I am enough; I strive to spread this sentiment to all those I encounter.

I invite you to accompany me on this journey, as I aim to kindle inspiration within you to embrace your authentic potential and share love unconditionally.

***

Introduction

Life often writes our stories with unexpected twists and turns, and for myself, the narrative was shaped by a series of harrowing experiences that left an indelible mark on my psyche. From a tumultuous childhood marked by instability and abuse to facing the insidious grip of shame, this essay delves into the life of a woman who endured pain and adversity yet emerged as a beacon of hope and resilience.

The Roots of Shame

Born into a world of uncertainty, my early years were marred by the absence of a stable father figure and the stress that my young mother shouldered as a result. The phenomenon of my stunted growth as a child was attributed to my mother's stress, foreshadowing the emotional connection and co-dependency that resulted from our struggles. As my mother, my sister, and I moved from place to place, our lives intertwined with various male figures; some brought kindness, but others only deepened my sense of shame.

Dark Shadows of Childhood

My childhood innocence was shattered in the face of traumatic experiences that would forever leave scars. At an age when games and laughter should dominate, my world turned sinister when I was coerced into inappropriate acts. These events, coupled with vague memories of male encounters led to night terrors and an overarching sense of shame. Other acts of abuse further shadowed my young life.

A Brutal Collision with Reality

As adolescence emerged, a new chapter unfolded, one marked by the harsh reality of judgments and social structure. Entering a new junior high school, I encountered cruel words that cut deep, exposing the harsh divisions of socio-economic status. The simple realization that we were different, poor, and vulnerable, evoked an overwhelming sense of shame.

Longing for Acceptance

Seeking some rest from constant turmoil, I turned to the possibility of family connections. The hope of finding solace within my father's extended family turned to ashes as our cousins distanced themselves, driven by perceptions of our worthiness to bear their name. This stark rejection not only echoed societal judgments but also added another layer of shame to my already burdened heart. I found myself riddled with doubts about my self-worth, plagued by a sense of inadequacy that was difficult to shake off. The persistent question echoed: *Why wasn't I sufficient just as I was?*

These thoughts became a dominant presence, eroding whatever remnants of self-esteem remained within me. In response, I embarked on a journey of constant effort, tirelessly striving to impress everyone around me, all in an attempt to prove my own value. It was as though I believed I had a duty to secure their approval. I didn't merely want to be liked; that craving had transformed into an unrelenting *need* to be liked, a compulsion that drove all my actions and decisions.

A Tumultuous Adolescence

My late adolescence was punctuated by yet another series of devastating experiences. A stepfather's abuse that robbed me of any sense of control and left me feeling powerless became an excruciating secret—one that I kept to preserve my mother's imagined happiness. Blaming myself for the struggles, my sense of worthlessness deepened, and my relationship with shame evolved, intertwining itself with my identity. This poor sense of self-worth had me dropping out of college, learning how to hide reality with alcohol, and procrastinating with the realization of any goals. The aspirations I did still have lessened with every poor choice that I made. I also found myself clinging to unhealthy relationships, believing they could fill the shame-fueled void in my heart.

The Anatomy of Shame

Delving into the anatomy of shame reveals its complexity. As a painful emotion, it manifests as a heavy cloak that overshadows one's self-worth. Consciousness of guilt, whether rational or not, becomes the breeding ground for feelings of inadequacy. Shortcomings, often self-imposed by unrealistic standards, amplify a sense of failure. Shame means we never feel like we are "enough." Impropriety, both real and perceived, further destroys self-esteem. The interconnectedness of these elements paints a comprehensive picture of how shame can engulf an individual's sense of self.

Reclaiming Power and Resilience

In my 40s, I found myself divorced and remarried, my life marked by a recurring cycle of self-destructive habits. Yet, amidst the turbulence, it felt as if divine intervention itself extended a lifeline of courage to me. Urging me to transform my path. Recognizing the need for change, I resolved to seek healthier ways to cope. The journey began with a resolute decision: I would give up drinking. While alcohol momentarily dulled the pain and cast a fleeting illusion of solace, it inevitably spiraled me into more destructive behaviors. That moment of relief would give way to deeper pitfalls, and each time, I sought solace again in the very thing that had led me astray.

But there finally came a time, guided by newfound determination, when I embarked on a mission to not only relinquish the crutch of alcohol but also to confront the underlying issues—the failures, the elusive goals, and the negativity that had haunted me. It was a pivotal moment, the first step toward forging a path to knowing that I am enough and lasting transformation.

A glimmer of hope emerged as I began this journey toward self-discovery and empowerment.

Through my journey to sobriety, I found peace and strength in my faith in God. As I confronted the empty void that alcohol had once filled, I came to realize that I was never truly alone. God's presence in my life became the steady companion I had longed for. With His guidance and unwavering support, I found the courage to break free from the grip of addiction. Each day became a testament to His grace, as the void within me gradually filled with a newfound purpose and a deep connection to my spirituality.

Through this divine intervention, I was able to overcome my struggles with drinking, and I now walk a path of sobriety, gratitude, and faith, knowing that I am never alone on this journey. My sobriety date is July 4, 2010.

I ultimately returned to college and obtained my bachelor's degree just a few months before turning 50. The truth is, it's never too late to change your trajectory. I aspire to inspire others who have faced hardships, assuring them that they are complete just as they are. Over time, I've cultivated wonderful and nurturing relationships with my husband, children, mother, and friends. Letting them be who they are, while not minding what they think of me. At age 53, I've embarked on a career path I never imagined possible or deserving of.

My story underscores the importance of recognizing that mistakes do not define a person's essence. This realization is a rallying cry to extend unconditional love and mentorship to individuals emerging from traumatic experiences, such as incarceration, institutionalization, battling addiction, or domestic violence. By transforming the narrative and rewriting their stories, we can disrupt the cycle of shame and build a future of strength and self-worth.

Conclusion

My story summarizes the profound impact that early trauma and shame can have on an individual's journey. Through hard self-reflection and with the support of the strong individuals in my life, I am becoming the woman that God wants me to be. I can only hope that my triumph over adversity serves as a testament to human resilience and the potential for healing and empowerment. Through empathy, support, and collective efforts, we can rewrite the stories of those who have been silenced by shame, reminding them that they are enough and deserving of a future defined by strength, self-love, and triumph.

WEATHERING THE STORM

Renee Storms

Who am I today?

Well darling let me tell you who I am now. I reckon I'm a mighty strong woman full of grit and determination. I'm a proud mama of five precious children and a darn good creative real estate agent in Fort Myers Florida. It means the world to me that I am free to wake up every day and do what I am passionate about. My career is about the lifelong relationships I build while helping people navigate the biggest decisions of their lives—buying, selling, and investing in real estate.

One thing I hold dear in my life now is prioritizing self-care and setting healthy boundaries. After weathering many storms, I have come to recognize the importance of taking care of myself. This commitment to self-care is a must and it allows me to show up fully in all areas of my life. I am dedicated to serving the community and supporting and empowering women. By being my authentic self, I create a safe space for women to share their stories and experiences as I'm empathetic and understanding.

I have experienced jaw-dropping events, so those who confide in me will find themselves within a judgment-free zone. I'm able to connect deeply with others offering support and holding space for them to be comfortable in their own skin. Life has taught me plenty, and I'm grateful for every lesson. I will continue to grow and learn. I believe that each day is a new chance to shine and a new opportunity for growth and connection.

***

My earliest memories of my childhood were marked by instability and uncertainty. My divorced parents would meet at the Florida-Georgia line to hand my sister and me off, a routine that became all too familiar—so much so that I often joke that I should be called the Florida-Georgia Line Girl. We never knew from one year to the next where we would live, or which school I would end up in. It felt like a constant cycle of starting over.

During those early years, my granny played a significant role in my life—she basically raised me. Whenever I was with her, I felt a sense of stability and affection. It was the safe and loving environment that I was craving.

Middle school was a whole different story. It was a challenging time for me socially. I longed for acceptance and just wanted to fit in so badly. My southern accent was not in my favor. I was called names to my face and behind my back. I won't mention who the ringleader was, but this girl really had it out for me and she successfully turned everyone against me. I found myself spending countless days alone crying in the bathroom stalls, praying to just fit in. God did shine a light on me when he gave me special friendships with Jocelyn, Lea, Melissa, and Mari. They didn't know it then, but they saved my life in middle school.

Even amid isolation and uncertainty, something within me began to take shape back then. I realized that I had a certain strength that could weather any storm. Like a diamond in the rough, I was being buffed and polished, preparing me to shine one day. I discovered that I thrive with authentic relationships and could adapt to just about any situation.

As high school approached, my overachieving mentality kicked in. I was determined to overcome the challenges I had faced. I enrolled in summer school, night school, and any other opportunity to earn extra credits. I was determined to graduate early and against all odds, I succeeded and graduated high school in three years. I started behind the eight ball due to my late birthday and not passing first grade. I found myself driving to school as a freshman—as cool as that was, it was also embarrassing.

By the age of 22, I was ripe for picking, vulnerable, and lacking self-worth. Past traumas, combined with my empathetic nature and a fear of conflict, led me into the arms of a narcissistic partner. Besides being manipulative and controlling, he was also a career criminal and was in and out of prison the first five years of the marriage, even missing his son's very first birthday.

Over the course of the 15-year marriage, I gave birth to five children, endured four miscarriages, and experienced waves of anxiety and depression. I had multiple nervous breakdowns. I was quickly swept up into his bipolar storm. There was a time when I joined him in his addictions, and that nearly killed me. I remember a time when my immune system was so weak and depleted that I ended up with shingles. I recall telling my sister I felt like an 80-year-old woman as I was crawling up the stairs because my body hurt to even walk, which prompted me to wonder...

HOW THE HELL DID I EVEN GET HERE?

Even in the darkest moments, I still felt a glimmer of hope. I knew God was watching over me, and I realized he was caring for me... in the palm of his hands. My ex-husband's constant absences on trips went from a few days to a few months at a time. That ended up being a blessing because it allowed me to start healing and discovering pieces of my true self coming back when he was gone. I was finally starting to see glimpses of happiness and hear the sounds of laughter from my children and myself; we were no longer walking on eggshells all the time.

During our marriage, it became painfully obvious that he was having multiple affairs, so I started tracking him. We had just recently moved and were supposed to be "starting over." He took one more trip out of town and I almost didn't track him. I guess I just wanted so badly to believe that he was really done with all of that running around and was really going on a business trip.

My curiosity still got the best of me. I ended up looking at my phone to see where he was. Sure enough, he was making a pitstop in Georgia at the Pink Pony strip club, picking up his 19-year-old pole-dancing girlfriend so they could head to California. I'll never forget the feeling of pain and heat coming from within my veins that shot up from my toes all the way up my body to the crown of my head. My sister was living with me at the time, I told her, *This. Is. It. I don't know how we'll do it, but we are out of here.*

I surrendered to God with all I had. *Please help me,* I asked, *if you open the next doors for me, I promise to go through them and I will not look back.* With only $1,300 to my name, I rented the biggest U-Haul trailer my Cadillac Escalade with bald-ass tires could handle. We packed our mattresses, clothes, and everything with any value. We took off that evening and drove through the night to Florida. I remembered about a good hour in and each mile that passed I literally could feel my anxiety decreasing and I could breathe better. I recall hearing music for the first time in I don't know how long. I had sadly been living in fight-or-flight survival mode for years.

Once he realized we were gone, my ex-husband began to threaten me by saying that he would take the kids from me one by one. He did not waste any time on that matter. He managed to turn my oldest son Cameron against me, convincing him to move away at the age of 15. He brainwashed him so that Cameron stopped calling me Mom and didn't talk to me for three years. Over time, he witnessed his father's true colors and found his way back to me and our bond grew stronger than ever.

Life had more heartbreak in store. The unimaginable happened when I received the call that my son Cameron had passed away from fentanyl poisoning. The pain was unbearable, and it felt as if my world had crumbled once again. Yet through the depth of grief, I have found the strength to honor his memory and cherish the time we had together. In his memory, I began donating a percentage of each one of my real estate deals to a nonprofit fentanyl awareness organization.

Sadly, my ex-husband continued his patterns of manipulation, succeeding in turning my next child Dakota against me. Also, at just 15 years old, Dakota chose to live with her father. It was a painful and heartbreaking experience, but I refused to let it break me. I maintained hope that one day Dakota would see the truth and find her way back to me as well. Indeed as Dakota grew older and wiser, she saw through her father's lies and returned to me.

But this past summer, my ex-husband targeted my third child Austin who is autistic. His same ol' tactics of devaluing me and stripping away their innocence have caused extreme pain and heartbreak. Austin was easily convinced that life would be better living with him, without all the rules and structure we have within our house. He promised him that he would not have to finish High School if he came and lived with him, he could just get his GED. I made it to 16 with Austin and he would be in 11th grade this year. He has quickly jumped to action and is working on my fourth child Arizona at the young age of 12 who is starting to feel the effects of his manipulation.

The tipping point in my life all came down to Hurricane Ian. It flooded our home in Southwest Florida in September 2022, and we lost it all. Every single trauma, pain, hardship, and all the never-dealt-with emotions came flooding out. It was now time for me to sift through them and feel it all. I remember being told as a young girl to "get over it," and "suck it up." At other times, I even heard, "It's not about you anymore, it's about your kids."

I'm here to tell you that it *is* about you, and your body keeps the score. At the end of the day, I now truly believe that Hurricane Ian was a blessing for me, as it stopped me in my tracks, forcing me to take action and begin my long overdue healing journey. I am a different person, and I am healing and reparenting my inner child daily. My healing regimen consists of weekly talk therapy along with Eye Movement Desensitization and Reprocessing (EMDR), journaling, acupuncture, traditional yoga, and clean eating/juicing. I've also been practicing Kundalini meditation, yoga, and breathwork weekly to fully awaken my potential and awareness. I now understand how to focus on living in the present moment.

Through it all, I remain steadfast in my love for my children. I show them love, light, and consistency, even in the face of adversity. I will not let my ex-husband's actions define our lives. I am determined to break the cycle and provide my children with the stability, love, and support they deserve.

As I write pieces of my life story, I open my heart fully, hoping to help other women who have suffered in silence. I want them to know that they are not alone and that they are worthy of a life they've always desired. With resilience, strength, and the support of others, we can overcome even the darkest of times.

FINDING MY LIGHT

Rebekah Alzada Barney

Rebekah A. Barney is the founder, owner, and president of the Southwest Florida real estate development firm, the Alzada Company, and developer of The Irving Downtown in the historic River District of Fort Myers, Fla. The names "Irving" and "Alzada" memorialize Rebekah's beloved maternal grandparents, Irving and Alzada Cross, who are still referred to as "Mr. & Mrs. Wonderful."

With more than 22 years of professional development experience and a personal dedication to the preservation and protection of natural and historical sites, Rebekah's previous developments include a $190 million historic renovation of Colt Gateway in Hartford, Conn.; more than 20 developments throughout The Bronx, NY; and several high-rises along the Caloosahatchee waterfront in historic Downtown Fort Myers.

Rebekah takes an active role in her community, and serves on several local boards and committees, including the Lee County Pace Center for Girls, HOPE Hospice, and the SWFL American Heart Association. In 2022, she was featured among the 100 Women to KNOW Across America, and in 2023, she was honored to be included among SWFL's top 10 Women in Business by *Gulfshore Business Magazine.*

Rebekah received a B.A. in mass media communications with a minor in economics from the University of North Carolina in Charlotte. An accomplished ballroom competitor and lifelong athlete, she loves to dance and plays a variety of sports, including volleyball, for which she was named Division I Academic Athlete of the Year while in college. Rebekah resides in Fort Myers with her husband, Jeff, and their four children.

***

I don't like the spotlight. It's too harsh, too humbling, too heavy. I'm always much more comfortable in the safety of the shadows—but I also learned early on that if I never push myself into the light, I'll never grow.

I was born under the umbra of two astronomically successful parents, and I orbited them in adoration with aspirations to be as great as they were. My mother holds multiple advanced degrees and distinctions, having just recently retired from a luminescent career changing lives through her work in the nonprofit world, but she's best defined by my memories of our early morning walks to the bakery for day-old bread and pastries to drop off at the homeless shelter or soup kitchen where we volunteered.

My flair for numbers and ample ambition come from my charismatic father, along with a fiery sense of independence and a fearlessness for new adventures—odd, but not entirely incongruous traits for an introvert with little desire for being the center of attention—and both of my parents contributed to my intense work ethic, my competitive spirit, and my eclectic (and a bit eccentric) sense of humor.

My parents loved me and encouraged me, but I always felt overshadowed by my brilliant older sister, the brainiac of the family who was constantly spouting facts and contemplating complex theories I couldn't even begin to understand. Like the towering high-rises my real estate mogul father was buying and selling, my sister's ever-expanding intelligence and academic achievements loomed over me, and I felt compelled to compete with someone I just couldn't keep up with.

When our little sister was born, I officially became the "middle child" (an onus only other "middle" children can understand), and with one genius already in the family, fueling my intense need to achieve, I dedicated myself to something I knew I was already good at—sports! It gave me a chance to shine, and I became the all-star athlete of the family. But I still always felt, at worst, somehow less than, and at best, merely just good enough—a jack of all trades, master of none. Those feelings of inadequacy and inferiority still darken my mental doorstep more than I'd like to admit, and I'm still learning new ways to ward them off.

But things changed when I left home for college. Suddenly, there was no comparison to be made, and I didn't have to be someone's less impressive little sister anymore. I decided to reinvent myself and, literally overnight, "Becky" became "Rebekah." It was the dawn of a new day for Rebekah, a more sophisticated and studious version of myself. No longer content with being "just an athlete," I threw myself into my studies and dove headfirst into campus life—and it worked, just like flipping a switch (although I still cringe a little upon hearing a family member or old friend call me "Becky").

I became a champion college volleyball player and a competitive ballroom dancer, and I graduated with a degree in media communications. Despite my distaste for the limelight, I'd dabbled in modeling—talk about finding your light—and even considered becoming a TV news anchor or correspondent. Instead, I ended up behind the scenes of *Martha Stewart Living*, first as an intern, and then as a production assistant. Not long before the show ended (later becoming *The Martha Stewart Show*), an opportunity to work in my father's real estate business set me on an entirely different path.

It ignited new passions and pursuits for me, especially in working for the protection and preservation of historical places and natural spaces, and I discovered my natural gift for numbers came in quite handy when securing financing and government grants. My hard work was acknowledged when, at the age of 27, I was named among the Top 40 Under 40 in Connecticut by *Hartford Magazine*. Fast-forwarding to 2023, at the age of 44, I was included among an awe-inspiring lineup of Southwest Florida's most accomplished 10 Remarkable Women in Business by *Gulfshore Business Magazine*, and I was feeling the same way I felt at 27—a sense of shock comingled with excitement, bewilderment and a bad case of so-called imposter syndrome. It had to be a mistake. Do I even deserve these kinds of accolades? My family and friends would say "yes," but they're biased, and I'm my own worst critic; I always feel like there's more I could or should be doing.

So far, over the course of my career, I've worked on nearly $1 billion of real estate development in New York, Connecticut, and Florida, always with my father. But in 2021, intent on blazing a new trail all on my own, I stepped out of his long shadow and founded the Alzada Company (pronounced *al-ZAYD-uh*). My first project, an eco-friendly rental community called The Irving Downtown, is currently in development in downtown Fort Myers,

Fla., and while there have been plenty of obstacles and challenges so far, it's thrilling to see it actually happening.

However, not long after I started my company, I suffered a heartbreaking miscarriage, and I suddenly found my bright new path obscured by a cloud of confusion and sadness. Should I focus on building my new business or on trying for another baby? I knew I wanted both—destination acquired—but how to get there? And would I be taken seriously as a pregnant CEO? Could I actually do both? Doubts crept in with these questions, echoed and amplified by judgmental comments (whether intentional or not) from peers and colleagues—comments made only to me, never to my working husband.

Ultimately, I thought about what I would regret more—not following my dreams and staying in the shadows, or temporarily worrying about attracting glares and glib gibes from others. With hope as our guiding light, my husband and I embarked on our IVF journey, and after many prayers, tears, and hormone injections, we were blessed with our fourth child.

My father never knew his father, and he didn't meet his biological mother until he was in his late teens. He was raised in extreme poverty by an elderly "aunt" of no familial relation, and after more than 50 years in real estate development, he's lived a real-life rags-to-riches story. He was young but already very successful when he met my mother, a new college graduate in her first year as a high school English teacher—and one of six kids raised by my wonderful grandparents in a humble but loving 500-square-foot home in New England.

Those beloved grandparents, Alzada and Irving Cross, whom I named my company and first solo development after, showered me—and each other—with joyful unconditional love. Their innate kindness and caring nature have passed down the generations, through my wonderful mother, and I see it in my own children, which is indescribably heartwarming. I recognized those very same traits when I met my husband and his family—in fact, I'm pretty sure I knew as soon as our second date that he was the one for me, my lifelong partner, my forever love. I learned from my grandparents' long happy marriage—and my own parents' less-than-happy marriage—that providing love and affection is a conscious choice, and I knew I wanted my home to be one of security, support, and unconditional love.

By all outward appearances, my parents built a fairytale home for us, but like any interesting story, nothing was exactly as it seemed. Memories of this time in my childhood glitter in my mind, and even though it wasn't always perfect, we had everything we needed and so much more—and we flourished. And though we lived in beautiful homes and attended good schools, many of my most luminous memories come from simple times spent with my grandparents, singing silly songs or tinkering with whatever project Grandpa Irving was working on. They lived with us for several years when I was growing up, and their unwavering love and support was formative for me. I think of and miss them every day.

My sisters and I grew up privileged but grateful, and fully aware that few people had the same kind of opportunities we did. When my parents' marriage ended, it came as a surprise at the time, but even as an adolescent I knew it was for the best, and eventually, it allowed me to develop closer relationships with both of them. They're both very generous people, each in their own way, and it's a trait I've gratefully inherited—a gleaming guidepost for how I live and move through the world. But the cosmic wheel of fortune is always turning, and just around the corner from every real estate market boom is a real estate market bust. My father wasn't invulnerable, and I was in high school when, in a flash, the grand and finely appointed houses we lived in were gone, replaced with smaller, simpler homes. It was all as quick as blowing out a candle—suddenly, the warmth of financial security had been extinguished. Fortunately, that boom-bust cycle eventually boomed again in my father's favor, and he bounced back by the time I was in college, but that "gone in a flash" feeling is seared into my memory, and it's given me a deeper appreciation for the many blessings in my life.

I can admit I'm a perfectionist, sometimes to my detriment, and I've also inherited proclivities for anxiety from both sides of my family. It was a struggle in my younger years, but with therapy and support and lots of self-reflection, I've learned—and am still learning—ways to overcome those anxious thoughts and feelings. I am blessed to have a wonderful husband and four wonderful children, and they are truly the eternal lights of my life, a constant glow in my heart and soul. But even their loving light doesn't make me immune to dark thoughts and feelings—I'm human. Sometimes I lose sight of my light, but I keep looking for it, and I keep going, maybe slower than usual, but I don't give up.

As I've gotten older and wiser, I've learned that it's simply impossible to be perfect, to know it all, to have everything figured out, and so I've grown more comfortable pushing myself into the spotlight (whether literal or metaphorical) because I've grown more comfortable with myself—my goofy, imperfect, always learning, always growing self.

One of the best pieces of professional (and personal) advice I've ever received is, "Never quit on a bad day." The shadows of stress and strife and sabotage and setbacks will always fall across your path, and there will always be more dark clouds gathering on the horizon, but that's life, and I've discovered that, when I live and love and work with good intentions, when I stop trying to control all those things and people beyond my control, usually, the light I'm looking for finds me!

THE HEALING POWER OF LOVE

Claribel Bocanegra

Claribel Bocanegra, born in Bayamón, Puerto Rico, is the founder of Gemstones in the Making and owner of Porto Fino Dental. Her practice has been taking care of SWFL's dental needs for the last 27 years. But Clary's passion extends beyond her practice. After arriving in Florida from Puerto Rico at age 15, she's consistently and passionately been involved in her community. Her most recent endeavors are founding LEAD Like a Girl! and most recently founding the nonprofit Gemstones in the Making.

In her spare time, Clary also volunteers as a mentor herself for young women in her community and, alongside her husband, funds scholarships for students to pursue vocational and higher education. Most recently, their dental practice, in partnership with

Gemstones in the Making, established a fund at Florida Gulf Coast University's (FGCU) Community Counseling Clinic for the participants of the program to receive free counseling and mental health services. She has participated in a multitude of Florida Gulf Coast University panels emphasizing the importance of diversity and the resounding benefits of creating an inclusive society that ensures equal opportunity for all.

She's an active member of the American Association of Dental Office Management. Clary is a devoted mother to her four children, Astrid, Isabella, Ricardo, and Alexandra, and a loving wife, sister, and cherished friend. Her passion comes from her experiences as a young, biracial, Spanish-speaking Southwest Floridian. She has experienced first-hand the challenges that young girls face as they take their first steps into adulthood—whether this is about mental health, their professional lives, or education opportunities.

She obtained her certified dental assistant training from the University of Florida, holds a fellowship from the American Association of Dental Office Managers, and has spent time learning from her peers, mentors, and friends. She has learned how collectively powerful we can be when we come together. Today, she hopes to inspire young girls to reach their dreams, whatever shape they may take. Whether they want to be cardiologists, yoga teachers, hair stylists, or senators, Clary hopes to inspire the next generation of girls to create a network of women who will fight inequality and support everyone so they may lead their lives proudly. She strongly believes that coming together is not just about charity. It is about building new futures where we no longer must struggle. A future where no one is left behind and we help each other RISE!! Futures where we can all have opportunities, where we can look to each other for help and to learn, grow, and SHINE.

**

I was born on May 22, 1977, in the town of Bayamon, Puerto Rico. My mom was just one month shy of her 16th birthday when she brought me into this world. I can't help but think about the emotions she must have experienced from the moment she found out she was carrying me in her womb. I have never asked her about that period of her life.

You see, our relationship is complicated.

There are many wounds in each of our hearts, but I know she did the best she could. She was raised by two alcoholic parents and had to take on the role of the mother figure in a household with six children. Pain permeated her life, carried over from previous generations, and steadily grew. I understand her journey was not easy. I've listened to a few accounts detailing the hardships she faced during her teenage years. Her own father attempted to sexually assault her (but never apologized for or acknowledged this, even on his death bed), and she was sexually assaulted and forced by my own father.

My father was older than her and very abusive.

I remember one night in our humble shared home. It was late. My baby sister, Glory, and my mom were getting ready for bed. Suddenly my dad, drunk and agitated, burst in, starting a heated argument. My mom screamed for my sister and me to hide under the bed, shielding us from witnessing the abuse. I quickly took my sister and concealed her under the bed, but then I emerged wanting to assist and protect my mom.

As I began walking toward the kitchen, I vividly recall locking eyes with my mother, and it was as if she had summoned the courage to stand up for herself. She swiftly grabbed a knife and began to defend herself. My father, in his drunken state, witnessed the rage that had suddenly welled up in my mother, prompting him to back off. Consumed by rage, my mom began to chase him, but before she went after him, she secured the door and left my sister and me inside the house.

I remember the fear of not knowing whether my mom would be okay, or if my dad would retaliate and harm her. In desperation, I screamed for help out of the window. I quickly grabbed a chair and had my sister crouch on top of it so that I could climb onto her back and attempt to open the door. After that, I distinctly remember the police taking my mom's statement while my father sat in the back of the patrol car. That marked the beginning of my mom's journey towards freedom. I can imagine the fear she must have felt, not knowing what would come next, and considering her limited resources and lack of family support.

However, I know that on that fateful night, as our eyes met, she summoned an inner strength. It was as if our souls connected, and the fear in my eyes ignited courage within her, lifting her spirits.

My mom has always been a fighter. I remember when we moved to the projects in Puerto Rico, and even though we didn't have much, we lacked for nothing. I now appreciate the fact that at a very young age, my mom did incredibly difficult things to ensure our survival. I know she carries these wounds deep in her heart, and I can feel them. I can see them. I can hear them. I often find myself contemplating what healing those wounds would look and feel like for her. Even though I understand all these things, I still harbor some resentment in my heart. I continue to grapple with reconciling her love for me with some of the choices she made. I try to remind myself that she did the best she could, and that she gave it her all.

When I look back, I see beyond the façade of the strong woman, flaws and all, to a young woman who was once so frightened. Yet, she managed to overcome her fears, pushing past them to create opportunities and a brighter future for her young daughters. Growing up with a single, young mother who was constantly in survival mode presented its fair share of challenges and consequences. Being the oldest, I often found myself in the role of caretaker, as my mom worked long hours as a sales representative. This meant we were home alone for extended periods of time.

At a very young age, I had to learn to cook, assist my sister with her homework, and essentially take on the responsibility of raising both of us. We were isolated, without the presence of grandparents to care for us, and our aunts and uncles were also struggling to survive, caught in the same family dynamics that surrounded us. There was no community to support us, and I can't recall any role models or figures I looked up to. My memories of childhood are scant, with only a few moments of joy that I hold close to my heart. I distinctly remember the happiness in those moments, all facilitated by my mom. We didn't have access to organizations like the Boys and Girls Club or other nonprofits that could provide resources.

However, there is one person I do remember. While I can't recall her face, name, or any personal details, I do remember that she genuinely cared. Every Sunday, she would gather the kids from the project into a circle and sing to us. The songs she taught us spoke directly to our hearts. I still vividly remember how she'd assure us that we were special, crafted with love, destined for greatness, and free to dream. She would say we could be anything we wanted, that we were born with a purpose. She planted those seeds in our hearts when I was just five or six years old. Those words continue to resonate deeply within me today, manifesting in phrases like "I am ENOUGH," "I am LOVE," and "I can achieve anything I dare to dream of."

It's as if I've heard those words before, like seeds that were planted and are now blossoming at a stage in my life when I need them the most.

You see, I have always struggled with my self-worth. I believe it's because of my life experiences, my feelings of abandonment and simply not believing that I was enough. During my teenage years, I grappled with self-confidence and my appearance. I attempted to engage in sports but never had the support necessary to fully commit. Surprisingly, I excelled in track and became a high school champion in Puerto Rico, despite having little to no training, as I had to rush home after school to care for my sister.

When I was 12 years old, my mother remarried. Her new husband was a very controlling man who was verbally and emotionally abusive. This only exacerbated my lack of self-worth while growing up. I wasn't permitted to ask questions; I was expected only to obey commands. Maintaining friendships was nearly impossible due to our frequent relocations, and I couldn't join clubs or engage in activities. I was constantly in survival mode. This way of living never allowed me to connect with myself or discover my true identity. It often feels as if I spent most of my life simply floating and bouncing through it. Perhaps that's why my memories, even of my adolescent years, are so scarce.

When I turned 16, my mom moved to the United States with my stepfather and my sisters. By that time, my mom had given birth to two more daughters with my stepdad. Unfortunately, when my stepfather lost his job, he decided to relocate with my mom and my sisters, leaving me behind with a complete stranger. Within the second week of living in her house, the woman (whose name I still can't recall, and I'm not even sure if we were related) informed me that I had to leave school and start working, or I would have to leave her house.

My mom wasn't sending any financial support, and she couldn't afford to take care of me. I was utterly shattered. I was an excellent student; I loved learning, and oh, how I adored books. I achieved the highest score on the SAT, administered by the College Board, among my high school peers in Puerto Rico. I aspired to be the first college graduate in my family, but that dream had to be postponed, and it left me feeling deeply frustrated. My anger overwhelmed me during that period, leading me down paths that no young woman should ever have to navigate just to survive. I felt utterly alone, abandoned, and unworthy of love or compassion.

I wandered angry through life, trying to please others and seeking approval. I became a chameleon, adapting to different situations, but in doing so, I wasn't truly living.

I turned to religion, but it only reinforced the belief that I had to conform in specific ways—dressing a certain way, speaking a certain way, participating in the church, and adhering to all the rules—to be considered worthy of love. In that environment, women were expected to live in submission, even when facing abuse. We were conditioned to remain silent, to be nice, and to serve—not out of love but as an obligation.

Breathing and living in that space became unbearable. Control was the ultimate law, and breaking any of those rules meant losing your worthiness of love and compassion. You'd face discipline and be cast out from what they referred to as the "family of faith." Navigating that environment was extremely challenging.

Summoning the courage to rise and embark on a journey of unlearning the narratives that had conditioned my mind was an immense challenge. It ranks among the most difficult things I've ever undertaken. I had to learn how to detach my self-worth from both religion and the opinions of others. This remains a daily struggle for me, even to this day.

All the examples I had from the women I grew up with were rooted in the belief that women must sacrifice themselves for their families. We were conditioned to put ourselves last, forsaking our own dreams and aspirations. In this context, marriage was often seen as the ultimate achievement, and dreams were dismissed as mere fantasies. This is a narrative I've only recently begun to deconstruct.

It's not easy, as those narratives are deeply ingrained. Breaking free requires a lot of introspection and embarking on a journey of self-love. This path has allowed me to step into my power, find my voice, trust myself, and understand that I need no one else's permission. I own my affirmations, I own my dreams, and I am the architect of my life.

This journey is not for the faint of heart; there are moments of deep fear. However, pausing to understand and question those fears is crucial to breaking free. It's a struggle, but I've discovered that the more we learn and shape the person we are and want to become, and the deeper we fall in love with ourselves, the easier it is to embrace our authentic selves and our power.

The freedom I've experienced with every step is like fuel for my soul. I won't deny that this process can be challenging and filled with friction, but the view from the top is breathtakingly beautiful.

There was a time when I genuinely questioned if I had the capacity to persevere through this process. I wasn't certain if I was truly prepared for the challenges of personal and spiritual growth. The prospect terrified me because it meant I had to believe in my own worthiness of all the goodness in the world—worthiness of love and abundance. It meant trusting that both God and the Universe desired a joyful and abundant life for me.

Even today, I still grapple with fear, and I encounter growing pains along this journey. However, I've come to understand that going back is simply not an option. I harbor significant dreams, and I've heeded the calling. A passionate fire burns deep within my soul.

I often question whether I possess what it takes to persevere. Thoughts of the many times I might fail, the numerous mistakes I'll make, and the hardships I must endure to reach the other side and become the new version of myself that I'm continually shaping, flood my mind. Yet, I can't help but reflect on the fact that it's only through the hardships I've already endured that I've gained the strength needed to be where I am today. I now welcome every opportunity, every failure, and every mistake as a chance to bolster my courage and gather more strength for the next level.

Today, I can only express my gratitude to the incredible human who gave birth to me—a brave 16-year-old young woman who chose to rise with all of her being. She rose with her fears, limitations, pains, strength, and courage. Because she rose, the generation that followed her is better off. Because she rose, I have been able to continue the healing journey so that every generation after can thrive. It requires courage from all of us. It demands resilience and perseverance, but above all, it calls for the most powerful force in the world to facilitate healing: LOVE.

CLOSING

Sue Ryan

Sue's mission is to empower and embolden individuals to maximize the opportunities and potential change will bring. As a speaker, change strategist, author, executive coach, caregiving coach, and mentor, she lives this through two passions of her purpose. She guides and inspires leaders and emerging leaders committed to business growth and next-level leadership to be great leaders of themselves and others. She guides non-professional caregivers to become confident, balanced, and supported in all phases of their caregiving journey.

Sue specializes in helping individuals and teams thrive during times of change. She works with them to clarify, align, develop, and implement solutions in highly competitive markets, while helping them create a culture poised to face the challenges of change with resilience and right action in the direction of their goals. Together, they successfully deliver long-term brand growth and value. Whether change is due to external factors such as market shifts, technology innovation, economic changes, or setting their sights on growth and expansion, understanding the dynamics and psychology of change enhances their ability for success. Sue delivers these through her signature offerings Intentionally Navigating Transitions—Leadership Through the Dimensions of Change™, The Prodigy Zone™, Leadership C.A.R.E.S.™, and The Caregiver's Journey.

Sue's corporate career of more than 30 years was in enterprise application software sales to companies across industries including healthcare, financial services, information technology, manufacturing, hospitality, and utilities. She was responsible for ensuring individuals were poised for change and their organizations were positioned for predictable success. While her performance was consistently recognized in the top tier, her most satisfying achievement was her nearly 100% client retention rate.

Sue has been in roles of family caregiving support for more than 40 years. She's moved from feeling frustrated, overwhelmed, and yes, sometimes frightened, to confident, balanced, and supported, navigating the transitions in her life, her care receivers, and those who support them on their journey. As a speaker, coach, author, educator, and mentor, she shares the lessons, tips, and strategies she's learned to help others positively navigate their caregiving journeys.

Sue has been a volunteer mentor of emerging leaders for Menttium since 2011. Sue volunteers in the children's ministry of Gulf Community Church, is a member of the Blue Zone's Engagement Committee, and is a passionate technology educator for seniors. Sue is a member of the International Coaching Federation.

Through her coaching, Sue earned the John Mattone Platinum—Elite Executive Coach ranking. Sue supports the

Leadership Collier Foundation and is a 2023 graduate of Leadership Collier. She volunteers as a speaker and community educator for The Alzheimer's Association and is a speaker and volunteer for AlzAuthors.

She has authored or co-authored three international bestselling books. Two are in the field of business. Her non-professional caregiving book is *Our Journey of Love: 5 Steps to Navigate Your Caregiving Journey.* She created the award-winning online course The Caregiver's Journey to support family caregivers through their entire caregiving journey. Sue recently gave her first TEDx talk. Next stop, the TED platform!

Sue's life motto is, "Go confidently in the direction of your dreams! Live the life you've imagined." ~ Henry David Thoreau

***

Wow! I feel like this book could have come with a warning: "Hold on tight... you're about to go on the emotional ride of your life!"

In the opening of *Slaying SWFL*, speaker, author, and interconnected wellbeing advocate Christin Collins defines women who are "slaying it" as: "Women who are comfortable in their own skin."

As you read each chapter, you learned none of us started there!

I'm honored to have been asked to bring closure to our journey. Yours as you navigate your own journey through the experiences shared, and each author's as she shares her unique "phoenix rising" story—her life journey that led her to emerge as the strong, beautiful, powerful, amazing, perfectly imperfect woman she is.

In Greek mythology, phoenix is a long-lived bird that cyclically regenerates or is otherwise born again. Associated with the sun, phoenix obtains new life by rising from the ashes of its predecessor. Phoenix rises from the cloud of darkness, and from the sacred ashes of her honor. Great in fame as she was, before. Phoenix represents transformation, strength, and renewal.[1]

In my role as a sales leader, if I didn't make sure everyone involved was in complete alignment with our understanding of the words we used, we could underserve, misrepresent, or completely miss the mark on an opportunity. I suggest you do the same. As you consider how each of these stories inspires your life journey, get a clear understanding of which words were chosen, and why. It's helpful (and even necessary) to do this for the words we choose for ourselves and in conversation with others as well.

The word "slaying" is an excellent example of the reason for this clarity; it has a wide variety of definitions! They range from "killing" to "stamping out," "defeating" to "overthrowing," "destroying power," "delighting," and "feeling overwhelmed"— especially with laughter.[2]

Other definitions include being "amazing," "awesome," and "exceptionally impressive."[3]

When you saw the word "slaying" splashed across the cover of the book, what emotion(s) came up for you?

With each story, you were drawn into a unique and inspiring journey where the life circumstances of each author came together

---

[1] https://embrace-yourself-embrace-the-world.com/2019/01/06/what-does-phoenix-rising-from-the-ashes-mean/

[2] https://www.merriam-webster.com/dictionary/slay

[3] https://www.wordhippo.com/what-is/the-meaning-of-the-word/slay.html

to a key turning point: the moment when they clarified for themselves what "slaying" meant to—and for—their own lives. They bravely brought their own raw, candid, vulnerable stories of slaying, shared how this concept impacted them and continues to transform their lives today.

How did each story clarify what "slaying it" means to and for you?

As you walked with each author through their story, perhaps you related to their struggles, their pain. Perhaps you related to their feelings of fear, helplessness, hopelessness, frustration, lack of worth, shame, anger, rejection, depression, and how they faced judgment. Perhaps you related to the choices they made to dull their pain. Perhaps you related to their moment of truth, the powerful and decisive moment when they made the choice to believe in themselves even when they had so little self-faith. Perhaps you related to the beginning of their life transformation as they developed their own unique resilience, using it to help them get up again and again until they became strong enough to make wise choices they hadn't previously had the capacity—or courage—to either make or sustain.

Whatever brought you to this book, it is our sincere hope that sharing our stories touches your life so you step into being the strong, beautiful, powerful, amazing, perfectly imperfect woman you're meant to be.

Today, I feel incredibly blessed and filled with gratitude. I believe everything in my life happens *through* me, not to me. I've learned each experience in my life has purpose—even if I don't understand or appreciate it in the moment.

I recently gave a TEDx talk about a perspective I created: massive acceptance and radical presence. They include the gift of living our lives without judgment of ourselves, others, or our experiences, so we're able to capture each experience for its ultimate purpose. I explain: "In the moment of an experience, we cannot possibly know if it is ultimately good or ultimately bad."

Accepting exactly what is, we're able to stay radically—that is, fully and completely—present in the moment. We have access to making our wisest choices even in the most challenging experiences and see joy even in the tiniest moments.

How did I get to this phoenix rising story in my life so now I'm joyfully slaying my life?

As I studied to make sense of many experiences in my life, I explored, with unquenchable curiosity, their purpose. I grew up in a family where my dad was incredibly kind yet non-confrontational. My mom lived with bipolar disorder, and the medical community couldn't treat it effectively, so she self-medicated with alcohol. I have an older brother I love and adore. He's brilliant and creative, and we often cannot understand each other.

I lived never wanting to let my dad down. (I'm using the word "never" correctly here. I know we're not supposed to write in absolute terms, yet I truly *never* wanted to disappoint or let my dad down. He could simply look at me with disappointment in his eyes, and I would be shattered.) He was very humble. When I was a child, he taught me not to "brag" about my accomplishments to not make anyone else uncomfortable.

Oh yes, I totally misunderstood that one for years!

I also lived trying to keep my incredibly artistic and creative mom happy. I continuously looked for what to do to keep her from spiraling, not knowing that from moment to moment she didn't know. I would always be trying to find and fix the "next shoe" —the next thing that would set her off. For much of my early life, I felt like a failure, because so often I couldn't figure out what would set her off. I would replay experiences over and over, exploring what I "should" have done.

I would keep trying harder and harder, thinking, *if only I'd...* (*fill-in-the-blank*).

My brother and I are naturally wired to see our worlds differently. Rather than being helpful, I often frustrated him. I love him truly and realize that not being in his life helps his life be more at peace. This brings me peace.

It's reasonable I had very little self-identity; I was continuously trying to be what others wanted me to be—feeling like I "should" be more like x or y. No matter how successful I became, I always saw my flaws and felt responsible for my failures instead of pleased with my success.

My *aha* moment—and it was just that—came in my thirties. I rarely took any time off work. My chosen field of information technology had few women in it at the time, and (it's OK to laugh at what I'm about to say... I certainly do these days!) I was afraid if I took time off, I would either be seen as weak, or they would see they could get along easily without me.

I decided to attend the Optimum Health Institute in Austin, Tex., for two weeks. They accurately describe it as: "A place to explore physical, mental, emotional, and spiritual well-being. Enable transformation so that you can achieve **optimum health**."[4] The entire experience focused on me! Through questions

---

[4] https://www.optimumhealth.org/ohi-austin

I'd never explored, I was invited to consider perspectives about my life I had previously been unaware of. I was given permission to celebrate my accomplishments. I learned how to see outcomes that were not what I anticipated as opportunities to learn from, rather than failures. I learned how to become stronger and use my unquenchable curiosity to explore with boundless energy.

Several days into my time there, after multiple sessions of guided personal exploration, our group came together one evening for a burning bowl ritual. We were each asked to sit quietly for a few moments and think of one thing we wanted to release in our lives to make space for new beginnings. We were given a small strip of paper and a pencil. At this point, after several days of reflection, I had thing after thing that came to me to write.

I finally settled on one. When it came time for me to drop mine into the bowl, I began sobbing uncontrollably. The room remained silent. Others also began sobbing, and we sat in our respective pain. The person next to me dropped her paper into the bowl. When everyone had put their pieces of paper in the bowl, our guide lit the papers, and we watched what we wanted to release literally go up in smoke.

After that, we were given pads of paper to write down all the things we'd thought of and hadn't written down. We were asked to continue recording as we thought of them throughout the rest of our time there. On our last evening, we had a bonfire outside and each of us put our lists into the flames. This experience transformed my life.

My unquenchable curiosity led me to understand why each of us in my family saw the world so differently. I began studying

Enneagram.[5] It opened for me an exciting world of understanding, permission, and perspective into why we view the world differently, how to embrace it, and how to use it to become the best versions of ourselves. I encourage you to explore as you slay your life!

"Each of us is a treasure in our world. When we know the gifts of our treasure, we transform our world by sharing them. Not why you, why not you?"

~ Sue Ryan

---

[5] https://www.truity.com/blog/enneagram/what-is-enneagram#:~:text=Definition%20and%20Meaning,types%20relate%20to%20one%20another

ABOUT THE CURATOR, LEIGH M. CLARK

Leigh M. Clark is on a mission to make an impact and live her legacy. From her busy career transforming businesses through technology, to her charity that throws around kindness like confetti, everything Clark works at is about making a difference.

Clark is an author with several Amazon bestsellers such as Living Kindly and The Dream is in Your Hands. She is embarking on a new series Slay the USA which features powerful women with purpose from cities across the United States.

Additionally, her nonprofit Kindleigh has made a significant impact nationwide in efforts such as painting and donating murals to other nonprofits, gathering school supplies for foster children, distributing crucial items to the homeless, delivering gifts to women and children who are victims of abuse and human trafficking, and paying off holiday layaways for strangers. Their work has been featured on Rachael Ray, The Today Show, and on many other national media outlets.

She is also a motivational speaker who has been featured nationally, including multiple times on the TEDx stage. Her hope is to inspire others to live their best life by sharing their own positivity. She believes that we can make the world a nicer place, one act of kindness at a time. Through helping to uplift others she has found her purpose and is leaving an indelible mark.

www.ingramcontent.com/pod-product-compliance
Lightning Source LLC
Chambersburg PA
CBHW061154120626
46546CB00005B/2066